P9-DHI-064

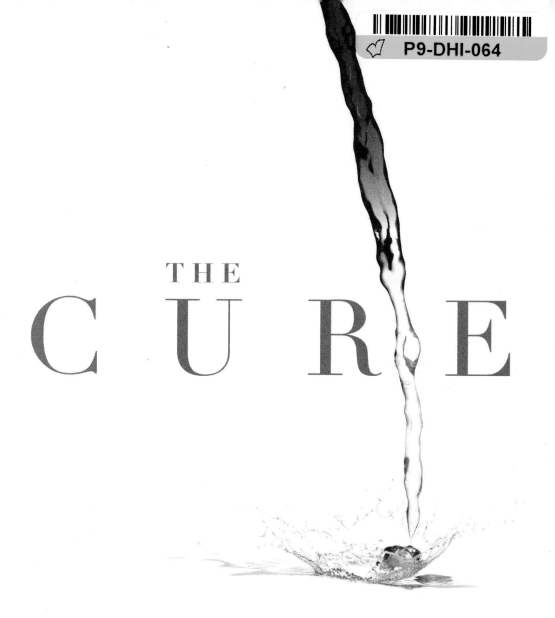

THE
CURE

What if God isn't
who you think He is
and neither are you

JOHN LYNCH | BRUCE McNICOL | BILL THRALL

www.Trueface.org

This book is a work of fiction. Names, characters, places and incidents are the product of the authors' imagination or are used fictitiously. Any resemblences to actual events, locales or persons, living or dead, are coincidental.

Copyright © 2011 by John Lynch, Bruce McNicol, and Bill Thrall.

All rights reserved. Except as permitted under the U.S. Copyright Act of 1976, no part of this publication may be reproduced, distributed, or transmitted in any form or by any means, or stored in a database or retrieval system, without prior written permission of the publisher.

Printed in the USA
First Edition: October 2011
Third Edition: 2016

Published by Trueface
1730 E Northern Ave Ste 106
Phoenix, AZ 85020
602-249-7000

ISBN 978-1-934104-08-8

The Message:
Scripture taken from The Message. Copyright © 1993, 1994, 1995, 1996, 2000, 2001, 2002. Used by permission of NavPress Publishing Group.

NIV:
Scripture quotations marked (NIV) are taken from the Holy Bible, New International Version®, NIV®. Copyright © 1973, 1978, 1984, 2011 by Biblica, Inc.™

ESV:
Scripture quotations are from The Holy Bible, English Standard Version® (ESV®), copyright © 2001 by Crossway, a publishing ministry of Good News Publishers. Used by permission. All rights reserved.

NASB:
Scripture taken from the NEW AMERICAN STANDARD BIBLE®, Copyright © 1960, 1962, 1963, 1968, 1971, 1972, 1973, 1975, 1977, 1995 by The Lockman Foundation. Used by permission.

WHAT OTHERS ARE SAYING ABOUT
THE CURE

"Reading *The Cure* is like standing on the edge of a rocky cliff over a crystal blue lake. You watch with amazement as your friends leap off and splash into the cool waters below. You long for the courage to do the same. John Lynch, Bruce McNicol and Bill Thrall call us to take a leap with them into the blue, into our destiny, into the incomparable adventure of grace. What holds us back? Why do we hesitate? What do we have to lose? Teetering on the edge, *The Cure* comes along and gives you a gentle push."

Glen Keane
Directing Animator, Tangled, The Little Mermaid, Tarzan,
Aladdin, Beauty & the Beast, Pocahontas

"Time and again in the history of his dealings with his children, God has led us back to Scripture and its exposition, there to delve deeply once again into the depths of His grace. Somehow we seem to need this renewal every generation afresh. In this generation, *The Cure* is at the center of it. We learn of grace, we see it freshly and are astonished once again at who we are in Christ: 'saints who sin,' and no longer sinners striving to become saints. We stand with the Holy Ones of God, co-heirs with Christ, as beloved of the Father as is the Son. This book repays close attention and frequent re-reading, for after we look away, the aura may fade, and we may quickly persuade ourselves that such truths are too great for us, too exalted to be true. We need to be reminded: behold yourself in Christ! Rejoice!"

Michael O. Wise, PhD
Scholar-in-Residence, Chair, Department of Biblical and
Theological Studies, Northwestern College

"There is no other resource that has had such a profound impact on my life, other than the Bible, like *The Cure!* It has literally transformed my thinking about God's grace that has radically changed my relationships with my wife, my kids, my grandkids, and my friends, enabling me to trust God and them with who I really am! I truly do see them through a different lens. And it is so much more beautiful than the old lens! *The Cure* will rock your world if you allow yourself to catch it!"

Dave Dravecky
Retired Major League Pitcher, San Francisco Giants, Author of
The Worth of a Man *and President of Endurance with Jan and*
Dave Dravecky

"Grace—an exquisite word carrying the power of God for new-covenant transformation. But that power depends on seeing all the dimensions of grace. Their vulnerability and careful attention to theological foundation make *The Cure* a book to treasure. As you read with your heart and your life, you'll enter into the joy of your salvation!"

Gerry Breshears, PhD
Professor of Theology, Western Seminary, Portland, OR

"Sometimes a book can change your life. This one changed mine, and I am still learning from it. This is the best and most practical book on living by grace that I have ever read. This is the rarest of books."

Dr. Roberta Hestenes
International Minister of World Vision, Former President of
Eastern University

"This book has revolutionized my marriage, my friendships, the way I write songs, the way I see this life in Christ. It has turned my world upside down!"

Bart Millard
Lead Singer and Songwriter, Mercy Me; including I Can Only Imagine and Flawless

"This is the most important expression of the gospel I have ever read. I'm a little too old and a lot too cynical to be swept away by the latest fad in Christendom. But God rocked my world through *The Cure*. I want to spend the rest of my life teaching and investing in these truths."

Dave Burchett
Author of When Bad Christians Happen to Good People

"I was captivated from the first page as stories of Good Intentions vs. Grace unfold, encouraging the reader to deal with the conflict within himself. Bruce McNicol, Bill Thrall, and John Lynch take the reader on an incredibly creative and fascinating adventure in their book *The Cure*."

Dean Niewolny
CEO, Halftime

"*The Cure* reveals how you can stop pretending to be a 'good Christian' and start naturally acting like who you are in Jesus Christ. This masterpiece on the believer's new identity is passionate, creative, and scriptural. It's everything you want in a book—it leads you straight to God's truth, and you have an incredible time along the way!"

Andrew Farley
Bestselling Author of The Naked Gospel *and* God Without Religion

"From a psychological and theological perspective, *The Cure* is the single most important book that I have read. This is the most needed biblical message for our world today."

Dr. Bob Bernatz
Corporate Psychologist and Principal Consultant, The Table Group

"*The Cure* teaches the best process I know for developing a leader."

J Robert Clinton, PhD
Professor and Author, The Making of a Leader

"If you have struggled with unresolved life issues, *The Cure* is the book you've been looking for."

Dr. Joseph M. Stowell
President, Cornerstone University

TABLE OF CONTENTS

Chapter One | *Two Roads* 1
Chapter Two | *Two Faces* 17
Chapter Three | *Two Gods* 31
Chapter Four | *Two Solutions* 43
Chapter Five | *Two Healings* 53
Chapter Six | *Two Friends* 67
Chapter Seven | *Two Destinies* 81

Discussion Guide 95

Discussion Guide 1 97
Discussion Guide 2 101
Discussion Guide 3 105
Discussion Guide 4 109
Discussion Guide 5 113
Discussion Guide 6 117
Discussion Guide 7 121

Notes 125
Acknowledgments 141
About the Authors 143

CHAPTER ONE | TWO ROADS

"The Law makes rebels of people who want to love and be loved."

When you're young, the life ahead of you is a pristine, never opened book. It has that intoxicating new book smell. You've just cracked the cover, the pages are white and clean, and you absolutely know there's a grand story ahead. When you're very young, you could be a cowboy or a ballerina. In the glory of youth, you and your friends are dread pirates, widely adored pop stars, superstar athletes, gallant knights, or a queen whose rule is just and kind. Later, the fantasies fade, but the dreams become more focused. Maybe you'll be the first human being on Mars, or the doctor who cures breast cancer. The story is whatever you want it to be, and you're still in the opening pages of your great novel. You know, though, that the story will be great. You know you have a destiny, a purpose in this life. Some of those dreams are your own, it's true. But some of those dreams, those hopes of destiny, are from God.

As we grow older, some of those dreams begin to fade, washed in pain, cynicism and failure. The edges tatter, the thread grows bare, and sometimes the fabric falls away completely. Something unnamed repaints the horizon. The mundane, agonizing details of life build and build like bricks. Soon we are too weary of wrestling with our everyday existence to entertain grand visions of destiny. Even our relationship with God, which seemed so wonderfully beautiful and life-giving at first, dims.

We don't stop walking, but we may as well. What toxin is this that can turn a wide-eyed dream into a grinding drudge? It's as if

1

we all woke up one morning under a curse we couldn't shake. We push on, one foot in front of the other, but we stop wondering why. The next thing we know, we've got rocks in our shoes and lungs lined with dust. The curse is not a metaphor, though. The curse is a lie all of us buy into, sometimes suddenly, sometimes slowly, like a frog in a pot. The lie breaks our hearts, and it scatters us in different ways. Some of us find shelter in religious discipline. Some seek solace in cynicism and unchecked deconstruction. Some are driven away completely.

Then we place blame: on ourselves, others close to us, our religious systems, the government, fluoridated water, or God Himself. Some of this blame is valid, for sure. Some of the places that should have been safest perpetuated the lie the loudest.

Here is the lie, in two parts:

We do not see God as He is,
and we do not see ourselves as we are.

We all believe the lie to some degree. Suddenly, the road we've been journeying along splits. Which path do we choose? Well, that's tricky. Throughout all of history, the cure has never come in the form we expected.

. . .

I don't even notice at first. But suddenly the ten feet in front of me are going different ways. And, I realize I have no idea which way to go. I'm staring at the intersection, like this could make it go away. That's when I notice the tall pole with two arrows at the top pointing down each fork. What's written on them is even more confusing than the fork. One arrow, pointing left, reads *Pleasing God.* The one leading right reads *Trusting God.* You're kidding. I'm supposed to choose between these two? I'm not doing that. Choosing one means not choosing the other. It's like being asked to choose between your heart and lungs. What I want is a bypass. But there is no bypass.

I look up at the *Trusting God* sign. This has to be a trap, a trick question. It sounds good, but it doesn't give me anything to do. It's too passive. How will I make a difference? If God and I are going to be in sync, there's got to be something more than trust. If the issue is me, I'm probably not going to figure out my destiny simply by trusting that God can be trusted!

I move over to the *Pleasing God* sign, pointing down the path to the left. This has to be it! After all He's done for me, the very least I can do is please Him.

So I set off on the path of pleasing God, shaded by towering oaks. I'm encouraged to see this path is well-traveled, beaten level with the feet of a million travelers. Many of them, in fact, are still on the path. The first group I pass is a trio of buskers, strumming guitars and a mandolin. We nod to each other politely. A little while on, there's a family of five camping just thirty yards off the path, next to a brook. Even farther, a middle-aged couple basks in the sun by the side of the road.

"Hello!" I wave. "Will I see you later on?"

"Nope." The man is smiling, but firm. "We left the Room of Good Intentions some time ago. We can't see going back."

"Okay," I respond, confused. I'm not sure what the "Room of Good Intentions" is, but not everyone wants to please God, I guess. After a long while, passing many more travelers by the wayside, I see a giant building looming in the distance. It looks like a hotel. As I get closer, I can see there's writing in bronze lettering across the front: *Striving Hard to Be All God Wants Me to Be.*[1]

Finally. Something for me to do. I strive after success in my career. I strive after keeping fit. Why would it be any less with God?

I draw closer and notice a door. Above the doorknob, a small, ornate plaque is bolted to the heavy wooden door. *Self-Effort* it reads. Of course! God does His part, and I do mine. It's about time someone said it.

I turn the handle and walk in.

I'm stunned to find a huge open room filled with thousands of people. I scan the group, trying to take it all in. "So, these are the people really living for Jesus." Soon I notice there's a woman, a hostess maybe, standing next to me. She is immaculately groomed. Every hair is perfectly in place, her makeup accentuating her features, her smile is wide and toothy. Nothing about her seems out of place.

"Welcome to the Room of Good Intentions."

She says it clean and cool, like she's been greeting people all her life. There's just the tiniest little shred about it that's unsettling, but I'm so excited to finally be here I don't think much of it.

"You have no idea how long I've waited to find this place!" I return her smile, grasping her primly outstretched hand. I call out to the crowd, almost involuntarily, "Hey, how's everyone doing?"

The room goes silent. It's full of beautiful people, smiling people. Some of them wear elaborately crafted masks, which is great because I love masquerades. This looks like my kind of place. One man steps forward. His smile, like the hostess, is broad. His bleached white teeth look as if they had been lined up by a ruler.

"Welcome," he begins, shaking my hand firmly. "We're fine. Thank you for asking. Just fine. Aren't we, everyone?" A few in the crowd behind him nod, smiling along. "My kids are doing great and... um... I'm about to close some very lucrative deals at work. More fit than when I was in high school, I'm telling you. I'm doing just fine. Everyone here is."

Before I can reflect on how strange that sounded, the hostess asks how I'm doing. "Me? Well, to be honest, I've been struggling with some stuff. That's partly why I'm here. I'm trying to figure out..."

"Shhhhh," she interrupts me, putting a flawlessly manicured index finger to her lips. She reaches behind a podium and pulls out a mask, handing it to me. She nods her head with a curt smile, indicating I should put it on. I stare at it for a moment. Others in the room are excitedly motioning for me to do so. Slowly, I slide the mask over my face.

My next thought is, it might be best to back off on the self-revelation. I find myself answering, as if from somewhere far away, "You know, I'm great. I'm doing fine!" And everyone in the room smiles before returning to their conversations.[2]

This is the Room of Good Intentions.

The main entrance hall is massive and ornate. Winding stairways lead to upper levels, where cascading fountains are ringed with beautifully upholstered sofas and chairs. There are doorways leading to ballrooms, dining halls, and fancily appointed living quarters. Everything is white marble and gold leaf. It's gorgeous and opulent. Across the back wall, there's a huge, embroidered banner. *Working on my sin to achieve an intimate relationship with God,* it reads.[3] Finally, someone's saying what I've experienced all these years. Early on, when I first believed, He and I were so close. Then over time I kept failing. I'd do something stupid. I'd promise I wouldn't do it anymore. Then I'd fail at the same thing again. Before long, it felt like He was on the other side of an ever-growing pile of the garbage I'd created. I imagined Him farther away each day, with His arms folded, shaking His head, thinking, *I had so much hope for this kid, but he's let me down so many times.*

But looking across this room, I know now I can change all that.

This room—it's impressive. The decorations are nice enough, but you can feel the courage and diligence. You can almost taste the full-hearted fervency, the accomplishment, the head-on determination.

There's the Fortune 500 executive who has given away ninety percent of his wealth to charity. There is the lead pastor of a thriving network of churches, a dynamic communicator whose theological insights are heard the world over. I meet a girl, elegant even in her simple, worn clothes, who has devoted nearly all her energy to providing medical supplies to the Untouchables in Kolkata.

So many good-hearted people fill this room. They have devoted themselves to God, to studying His character, to pouring themselves into spreading His Word, to serving humanity in the name of Jesus. This must be it! Soon God and I will be close again.

Weeks run into months in this room, and a slight unease starts to creep in. It gets stronger by the day, but I can't put my finger on it at first. I'm noticing many in here talk in a sort of semi-joking, put-down banter. It's familiar, but a bit off. And standing this long on the edges of insider conversations, I realize I never noticed how annoying or obvious the subtle bragging sounds.

Even through those elaborate masks, I'm struck with how tired everyone looks. Many conversations are superficial and guarded. Several times, I've caught the real faces of people with masks removed when they thought no one was looking. There is a deep, lonely pain in their expressions.

I'm starting to think differently, too. The comfort I felt when I got here is fading. I'm carrying this tension, like if I don't measure up, I'll be shunned. Oh, and with God too!

Here's another thing: Despite all my passionate sincerity, I keep sinning. Then I get fixated on trying not to sin. Then it all repeats: same sin, same thoughts, same failure.

I spend more time alone now. It's hard to be in public very long before my mask starts to itch fiercely. I spend more time preparing to be with people than I spend actually being with people. I can't seem to do enough to make these people, or God for that matter, happy.

Increasingly, the path to pleasing God seems to be about how I can keep God pleased with me.

One day, it dawns on me what I've been doing to myself and to everyone around me. I've been trying to meet some lofty expectation, primarily to gain acceptance from people. I don't even know why I'm performing for them. To satisfy a God I'm not sure I can ever please? Even worse, I expect everyone around me to do the same.

. . .

There's no denying the appeal of the Room of Good Intentions. But, the room is predicated on a lie, producing many sad consequences.

For instance, when we embrace the path to this room, we reduce godliness to a formula:

More right behavior + Less wrong behavior = Godliness

There's only one thing wrong with the equation: It completely disregards the righteousness God has already placed in us. Yes, we mature in godliness, but if we disregard the righteousness that results from trusting what God has done in us, we're hiding who we truly are.

This path is cruel in its heroic-sounding deception, partly because it never allows us to see a fundamental truth:

We can never resolve our sin by working on it.

We may externally sublimate behavior, but we're essentially repositioning the chairs a bit on the deck of a sinking ship. When we strive to sin less, we don't.[4] Worse, the whole hamster-wheel effort of it all causes us to lose hope that anything will ever break through. In fact, this path actually seals us in immaturity. Even though this distorted theology breaks our hearts over and over and over, we desperately keep trying it.

What a wicked hoax.

.   .   .

Now I'm frantically working my way through the room, searching for someone—anyone—willing to talk about what's going on inside me. But nobody wants to hear it. It's as if they fear expressing my concerns will expose theirs.

So, even though I was certain this room might be my only real chance of getting it right, I find myself slipping out the door unnoticed. I thought I'd never leave, and I'm crushed.

A few hours later I'm sitting down at the grassy edge of the path, back at the fork in the road. That middle-aged couple is there, too, lounging on the other side of the path in the shade of a tree. The man smiles, with a hint of disillusionment; it's one of the more natural smiles I've seen in a while.

"That place is weird, huh? I'm glad we got out of that mess," he says, spitting out his words with a twisting smile.

I nod my assent, and he takes a deep breath before leaning back to join his napping wife.

Now what?

My eyes drift back up to that sign, and I read the arrow pointing down the road to the right. *Trusting God.*

I shake my head, look up, and ask the sky, "Is there a third road?" Nothing. Even the couple across the path is snoring. I sigh as I climb to my feet, brush myself off, and head down the right fork.

The path is rougher here, rutted and pockmarked with stones. It's a little steeper and slower going, but prettier, too. There are roughly hewn stone bridges over fast-flowing creeks and scenic vistas over vast, green valleys. After several hours, I see another huge building in the distance. When I finally reach it, I see these words emblazoned in tall bronze letters across the facade: *Living Out of Who God Says I Am.*

That's supposed to help me how? I've been trying to live out what God wants me to be this whole time.

Again, there's a huge wooden double door, and again there's a plaque over the knob. But this time there's only one word written over it.

Humility.[5]

Suddenly every effort of this entire journey collapses on me. Tears I've kept back so long well up as I mumble through my sobs, "I'm so tired. I can't do it. Help me. God, You're more wise, more right, and more loving. And I have not let You love me. I've fought so hard to impress You, and none of it did. Now I'm weary, empty, and alone. I'm tired of performing. I'm tired of pretending I can please You by any amount of effort. Help me, my God!"

After minutes in front of that door, I wipe my wet eyes and nose on my sleeve. I run my fingers through my hair and desperately pull myself together. If this is anything like last time, I want to make a good first impression, and puffy eyes and tear-streaked cheeks won't do. Finally, I reach for the knob.

Inside, it's much like the other room. The layout is nearly the same, though the décor is toned down. The gold leaf and marble are replaced by warm carved wood and polished stone. The intricate details in every adornment are conspicuously missing, replaced by tasteful simplicity. Instead of sofas draped in shimmering silk, there are overstuffed couches and chairs. There are also more windows. Natural light pours in and I can see the views outside are breathtaking. Glass doors lead out onto porches and decks scattered with Adirondack chairs. Another hostess approaches. Like the hostess in the Room of Good Intentions, she is gorgeous, but her beauty is natural. She smiles, and I notice her eyes are smiling too. I realize with a start that the other hostess never smiled with her eyes. In a voice as beautiful as anything I've ever heard, she says, barely above a whisper, "Hello. Welcome to the Room of Grace."

Then, with a pause and a smile, she clasps my hands in hers, "How are you?"

The last time I answered this one, I was handed a mask. This hostess is nicer, but I'm not convinced.

"Fine. I'm doing fine..."

The whole room is watching me now, and I see eyebrows tilted in skepticism. My heart sinks. I'm so tired of this. I turn toward the room, all eyes on me, and yell out so everyone can hear.

"Hey, everybody, listen up! I am not fine. Not fine at all! I haven't been fine for a long time. I'm tired, confused, angry and afraid. I feel guilty and lonely, and that makes me even angrier! I'm sad most of the time and I pretend I'm not. My life is not working at the moment! I'm so far behind and freaked out about what to do next, I'm almost completely frozen. And if any of you religious kooks knew half my daily thoughts, you'd kick me out of your little club. So, again, I'm doing not fine. Thanks for asking. I think I'll go now." I turn toward the door before I have a chance to break down again. As I grab for the knob, a voice booms from the back of the room. "That's it? That's all you got? I'll take your anger, guilt, and dark thoughts and raise you compulsive sin and chronic lower-back pain! Oh, and did I mention I'm in debt up to my ears? I also wouldn't know classical music from a show tune if it jumped up and bit me! You'd better get more than that little list."

The room erupts in warm, genuine laughter, and I know it's not meant to embarrass me. The hostess leans in, nudges me, and kindly smiles. "I think he means you're welcome here."

I step into a crowd of welcoming smiles. And there's not a mask to be seen anywhere. Right away, I wish I'd known these people all my life.

· · ·

You're in the Room of Grace! Grace! That word appears 122 times in the New Testament. The Judaizers in the apostle Paul's day hated it. They feared what it would do if it got loose. "Paul, you can't tell them this!" they said. "These people are immature, lazy and have little religious background. They'll abuse it as soon as they can. They'll live Christianity-lite. These people are weak and want to do whatever they want. And believe me, what they want is not good."

Paul responds, in essence, this way: "You'd have a great point, if it wasn't for two truths. First, these people have a new nature.[6] They have Christ in them.[7] They're not who they were. They don't want to get away with anything. They want to enjoy Him, and can't find a way to do that within your ugly system.

"Second, they have the Holy Spirit,[8] who is able to correct, encourage, rebuke, and challenge. They have God, you know."

If you're looking for compliance, you can get that without God. Just wield enough power and people will do what you want them to. At least as long as you're around. But when you're out of sight, eventually—inevitably—they'll revert to what they've been denied. The real trick is to allow the desires of the new heart to come out and have a run of the joint. We're hardwired for heartfelt obedience. We have to be religiously badgered into compliance, which leads to eventual disobedience. Only bad theology can do that. Sin and failure is all we think we have until new life is wooed forth. We need others to show us God beautifully, without condemnation, disgust, and unsatisfied demands. We long to obey Him. It makes our souls sing. We've just been goaded so long, we've learned to shield ourselves from religion. We'll fight that kind of authority just for the fight. It's what the Law does in any form.[9] It makes rebels of people who want to love and be loved.

There's an incredible phrase in Hebrews: "Without faith it is impossible to please God."[10] This statement shows us the path we must take. Only by trusting can we truly please God! If our primary motive is pleasing God, we'll never please Him enough and we'll never learn trust. Pleasing God is a good desire. It just can't be our primary motivation, or it'll imprison our hearts.[11] If all we bring to God is our moral striving, we're back at the same lie that put us in need of salvation. We're stuck with our independent talents, longing, and resolve to make it happen. This self-sufficient effort to assuage a distant deity—it nauseates God.[12]

When our primary motive becomes trusting God, however, we suddenly discover there is nothing in the world that pleases Him more! Until you trust God, nothing you do will please God.

At that point, pleasing God is actually a by-product of trusting God. Pleasing is not a means to our godliness. It's the fruit of our godliness, for it's the fruit of trust.[13] Trusting is the foundation of pleasing God. Lacking that basis of trust is like trying to build a house without a foundation.

The citizens of the Room of Grace get the privilege of experiencing the pleasure of God, because they have pleased God by choosing to trust Him. God has specific areas of our lives that He would like us to trust Him in, and looking for these opportunities is one of the best parts of the journey.

. . .

Eventually, I notice a banner in this room, too:
Standing with God, my sin in front of us, working on it together.[14]
I'm not sure I get it yet.

. . .

What if we could believe this is how God sees it, how it really is? What if Christ, for the believer, is never over there, on the other side of our sin? What if the power of His death on the cross allows Him to stand right in front of me, on my worst day, and smile bigger and happier than any human being ever could?

. . .

That night, my loud new friend shows me to my room. It is simple and comfortable. The warm glow of a reading lamp bathes the room in a welcoming light. I'm happily exhausted from a seemingly endless parade of introductions during the day.

"Sleep well," my friend says, patting my shoulder firmly. "We're so glad you're here."

I take off my shoes and rub my sore feet, overwhelmed by it all. I'm tired, but the good kind of tired, like when you know you've put in a full day's work. I think back on the banner I read, and suddenly I know what it means. Before, God was always "over there," on the other side of my sin, obscured by the mound of trash between us. But now I realize He's here, with me. I can picture it as clearly as if it's happening.

He puts His hands on my shoulders, staring into my eyes. No

disappointment. No condemnation. Only delight. Only love. He pulls me into a bear hug, so tight it knocks the breath out of me for a moment. At first, I feel unworthy. I want to push away and cry out, "I don't deserve this. Please stop. I'm not who you think I am!" But He does know. And soon I give in to His embrace. I hear Him say, "I know. I know. I've known from before time began. I've seen it all. I'm right here. I've got you."

And now I'm holding on with all my might. He stays right there in the moment, until He's certain His love has been completely communicated and received. Only then does He release His grip, so He can turn to put an arm around my shoulder. He then directs my sight to that mound of filth now out in front of us.

After several moments, with a straight face He says, "That is a lot of sin. A whole lot of sin. Don't you ever sleep?" He starts laughing. I start laughing.

Gazing at that mound of pain, I consider that I never thought I'd experience this kind of moment. All of the pain, regret and damage of my life are laid out in front of me. All that have caused shame and condemnation. All that have caused me to pretend and impress and yearn for control. All that have broken my heart and His. But now I'm viewing it with Jesus' arm around me! He's been holding me with utter delight, all with my sin right here in our midst, never allowing it between us. He wants to know me in the midst of this, not when I get it cleaned up. I know now that if this mound is to ever shrink, it'll be by trusting this moment for the rest of my life.

He looks back at me. "We'll deal with this when you're ready. I've got your back."

I search His eyes, barely able to comprehend this love. Then it's over, and I'm back in my room. I'm asleep the moment my head hits the pillow.

The next morning, over fluffy waffles and bacon thick as a pork chop, I tell my new pajama-clad friend about the realization, how real it felt. He nods, grinning wildly.

"Yep, it's something, huh? We all experience something similar when we get here." He stabs a slice of pineapple with his fork. He winks knowingly. "You've got a lot more in store."

. . .

Wouldn't it be great if we could always stay right here? Some do.

They never again leave the Room of Grace and all its stunning, panoramic, life-giving surroundings, except to intentionally rescue and stand with those still outside.

However, many choose not to stay. As absurd as it sounds, some never even give themselves a chance to choose, a chance to get there. You see, not all make it back to the fork in the road after leaving the Room of Good Intentions.

Scattered along the entire path back towards the fork, you'll find them. Some sit alone, tucked away, almost out of sight. Some collect in twos and threes. Many spend the rest of their journey there. The Room of Good Intentions broke and jaded their hearts, robbing them of hope. It made them so sick, they're nearly anesthetized to believing life can ever be different. Man-made religion has beaten them down. Many are oozing with apathy. They can think of no good reason to try; they simply don't care. Some of God's most passionate, gifted, and dedicated servants are despondent along that road.

These wounded express themselves in many forms. Some are cynical and smug, but it's a cover. They're self-protecting from vulnerability. They're still articulate and insightful—they just now speak from the fringes of the arena. They're bleeding from having risked vulnerability in a community that didn't know what to do with it. Some are bitter, lashing out at anything with more structure than an agreed-upon meeting time. Some create straw men, globalizing their enemies into generalized categories so they can ridicule them more easily.

When they do get together, they spend much of the time rehearsing their wounds. They talk about what they don't like. Their mantra is mistrust of any authority. They brag of being free from the bondage of religion, and they say this often in the same breath they rehearse their wounded identity. They can no longer remember the innocence of trust. They've seen too much.

For a season, what they are doing can be right and deeply corrective. They see from the vantage point of having little left to lose. But after a while, it makes them unforgiving, and there are now very few surrounding them who can help guide them to forgiveness.

No one matures in bitterness. No one gets free in isolation. No one heals rehashing the testimonies of bad religion. No one gets to love or be loved well in self-protection.

Self-protection is one of the great oxymorons. We're the only person in the world we don't have the potential to protect. And once we hide from trusting God and others, we become more enflamed, more self-justified, more calloused in repeating our blame.

The ones along the road are accurate about their pain. Their wounds are real. So real, in fact, they can't make it back by themselves to the fork in the road. They don't need an improved version of what they left. They smell manipulation in such an offer. Their senses have been heightened by pain. They too need the cure. Few destinies are more beautiful than the ones given to those who set out from the Room of Grace to find them.

The second reality is even harder to understand than the first:

Not all stay in the Room of Grace once they've been there.

The Room of Grace is tricky business for those who've believed self-made excellence makes the person. For not only must we believe we are accepted, we must also learn to accept the yokels already here and the rookies who come in fresh each week! Oh, generous executives, successful pastors, and social justice workers are here too. But, there is a vast difference. These made a life-altering choice back at the fork in the road. They're trusting who God says they are, instead of adding up their behaviors to prove their godliness. They're convinced they can never resolve their sin by working on it. They know their sin is never between God and them. They live in the truth that there are no "together people." They live careful and carefree because they realize the Father is crazy about them, on their worst day. They too, must learn to rest in the sufficiency of Christ in them. If they stop trusting these stunning truths, they'll soon return to the familiar, back in the Room of Good Intentions.

For those of us weary of pretending, weary of being weary, we've found our home in the Room of Grace. It's where God and I live together, along with all who dare to trust that God sees us this way.

Whenever you're tempted to think you don't belong, that you've failed too often, failed too big, or are not meant to be close to God—just then, someone, maybe sitting very close to you, will smile and kindly say, "That's all you got?!" It's their way of saying, "You're welcome here."

CHAPTER TWO | TWO FACES

"Soon, I was back to trying to impress a God I imagined was growing more and more impatient with me."

The day the hostess in the Room of Good Intentions handed me that mask, slipping it on felt very familiar. It felt safe. I'd been wearing one for a long, long time. I just wasn't aware of it.

Now, today, for the first time since before I can remember, I really believe I'm not wearing one. Just because I'm in the Room of Grace doesn't mean I won't put another back on, or so I'm told. But for today, at least, I think I'm me. Early this morning, I walked out on the balcony deck off the first floor of the main hall. I sat down in an Adirondack chair, watching the sky as the sun rose and melted off the mist. My face felt cool in the early morning air. I forgot how much I miss feeling God's presence. This will take some getting used to. But everything is alive, less rehearsed, a little vulnerable, incredibly hopeful.

Here's my question: If this life of Christ in us is true—if there is no condemnation, if He's perfectly working to mature us from the inside out and if He's absolutely crazy about us despite all our stuff— why would any of us ever put on a mask again?

. . .

I will—each of us will—be tempted to return to my mask each time I lose the confidence of my new identity.[1] Daring to trust who Christ says I am, who He says He is in me, even when I feel I least deserve it and the old shame sweeps over me—this is the only way to keep the mask off, to keep feeling the cool breeze on my face.

There are times when it seems like those of us who believe in Jesus are wearing more masks, and we seem to wear them more often than those who don't believe! What's with that? The truth is, we face even more pressure as followers of Jesus. We're tempted to don our masks even more if we haven't trusted our identity.

All of us are tempted to wear a mask when:

♦ We want to prove to others that we're worthy of their love.
♦ We want to prove to ourselves that we're worthy of being loved.
♦ We want others not to feel sorry for us.
♦ We fear if others see us truly, they won't want to know us.
♦ We want to be seen as great.

Believers in Christ additionally are tempted to wear a mask when:

♦ Our failures tell us the experiment of grace didn't work.
♦ We want to prove to God that we're worth His choice to love us.
♦ We believe God wants us to fake it so He looks good.
♦ We want God to make our life work and our behavior seems like the price tag.
♦ We think God cares more about right behaviors than our trust and dependence.
♦ We think we're in competition with others, graded on a spiritual curve.
♦ Our shame makes us believe we must assuage God's disgust in us.

Can you remember the first time you felt free enough to talk to God honestly? When you discovered you weren't hiding anything or pretending, no longer talking to Him in manufactured religious jargon? Maybe you'd just met Jesus, or maybe you first saw Him for who He truly is, in all His majesty, glory and goodness. It's a moment of freedom, and raw, unguarded hope like you'd never before imagined. It's like you could feel your own blood pulsing through your veins, so brightly alive! God waited an eternity for this moment. He knew He couldn't fully reveal Himself until He could cause you to risk trusting Him with who you really were. It was stunning. It took fear away. It broke lifelong patterns of dishonesty. People couldn't figure out what happened to you. You were wildly free, but safe. You were unguardedly alive, but more caring. You were full of life-giving joy, but more deeply sensitive to the pain in others. It painted your world in colors you didn't even know existed. I had this same experience. But something happened in the following months and years. I lost confidence that His delight and new life in me were strong enough to haul away that giant mound of rotted cat food and mayonnaise, the failures I presumed stood between Him and me. I could point to aspects of my life that weren't changing fast enough. So, I gradually bought the sales pitch telling me I'd have to find something else, something miraculous and mystical I'd receive if I could only prove I cared enough. I set about gallantly propping up my world.

Only now, because it was about God, the stakes were higher. I represented something other than just me, and the pressure was greater. Much greater. Soon, I was back to trying to impress a God I imagined was growing more and more impatient with me.[2] I learned to bluff, manipulating and managing my persona to appear better than who I feared I was.

No one told me this two-faced life would severely stunt my growth.[3] Or that it would break my heart. No matter how many titles and accolades I accumulate, I remain wounded and immature— long on "success," but short on dreams and substance. I admire people who live the Trueface life, but my loss of hope forces me to scramble for safety from behind a mask. The cost is horrific.

No one told me that when I wear a mask, only my mask receives love. We can gain admiration and respect from behind a mask. We can even intimidate. But as long as we're behind a mask, any mask, we will not be able to receive love. Then, in our desperation to be loved, we'll rush to fashion more masks, hoping the next will give us what we're longing for: to be known, accepted, trusted and loved.

This is no new phenomenon. Remember its source? God came in the cool of the day to be with Adam and Eve. He called out to a hiding Adam, "Where are you?" though He knew very well where Adam was. Adam responded, "I heard the sound of You in the garden, and I was afraid because I was naked; so I hid myself."[4]

Afraid. Naked. Hidden. These were the first steps of a dance we've been stumbling to ever since. We become afraid because something we did or was done to us makes us feel naked. This nakedness cannot endure remaining uncovered. Nothing is more embarrassing or vulnerable than nakedness. Not knowing another option, we hide ourselves. Our dance now follows nearly identical steps. This shame—this self-awareness of their "uncleanness"— prompted Adam and Eve to fashion masks from leaves to hide what they now feared was true about them. It wasn't just that they'd done something wrong. They were both convinced something was now uniquely and terribly wrong about them, with them. This is how shame works, and it's different from guilt. Guilt wants to lead us to forgiveness, to be cleansed. Shame drives us to hide, convinced we cannot truly be forgiven or made clean. It forced them and has forced us to cover ourselves with whatever is available at the time.

So Adam and Eve covered their nakedness with fig leaves. And it worked. No more shame, no more hiding. And they lived happily ever after...

Umm... no.

They still hid! This is the earliest recorded result of sin management. It will not work. It hasn't ever worked. When I discover I'm still hiding, that probably should be the hint that whatever I've tried to cover my shame with hasn't taken.

It wasn't until they trusted that God did something—provided His own covering for them[5]—that they could be free from hiding and condemnation. This is still true for me, many centuries later. Any time I hurt another or make wrong choices, the way home is not by attempting to cover my failure through something I can do to pay God off. The way home is not effort, not amends, not heroic promise. The way home is trusting what God paid to cleanse me.[6]

This life in Christ is not about what I can do to make myself worthy of His acceptance, but about daily trusting what He has done to make me worthy of His acceptance.[7]

Back to the garden. On that day, all humanity learned how to look over shoulders; to dart glances; to say one thing and mean another; to hide fear, deceit and shame behind a nervous smile. That day, we learned how to give the appearance we're someone other than who we actually are.

We begin to lose hope we can be "fixed." So we cover up. We put on a mask and begin bluffing. After a while, we can barely remember how to live any other way.

Mask-wearers fall into a variety of groupings. While there will always be endless variations, these three groups identify most of us.

THOSE TRYING TO CONVINCE OTHERS THEY'RE DOING "JUST FINE"

This crowd is convinced neat, hidden, and tidy are better than authentic and known. They believe God wants us to appear orderly and good, whether we are or not. The appearance of appropriateness and rightness is their highest value. Parents in this group applaud children more for pious behavior than for learning to trust God.

We are surrounded by nicely scrubbed folk who smile broadly and shake each other's hand firmly. Our conversations can go something like this:

> *"Hi, Enrique. How ya' doin'?"*
> *"Doin' fine, Sarah. Yourself?"*
> *"Fine, Enrique, fine. Couldn't be finer. Fine day, eh?"*
> *"Fine indeed, Sarah. Oh hi, Carmen. How ya' doin'?"*
> *"Well, hello, Enrique. I'm doin' fine. Can't complain. Fine day we're having. Yep, just fine."*
> *"Oh, yes it is, Carmen. Fine as fine can be. How's that husband of yours?"*
> *"Well, Enrique, he's doin' fine, too. Whole family's a big old basket of fine! Now, just so you can pray effectively, Mrs. Sanderson has it on reliable information that several other unnamed families are not doing fine."*
> *"Well, I'm sure they'll be fine, Carmen. What matters is that we're fine... just fine."*

This mask hides pain. It covers shame with appearance and a forced smile. We're convinced there is no real help for our issues and the best thing we can do is hide our true identities. If we thought it wouldn't ruin everything, we'd yell out, "You have no idea who I am! Nobody does! Not even my spouse! Even surrounded by friends and family, I'm unknown. When I enter a room full of people, I'm rehearsed. I can make small talk. I can even enter into deep intellectual discussions. But the person you see is made up on the run while the real me is frantically operating levers behind a mask."

If we could take off our masks long enough, many of us would say, "I'm tired. Really tired. I'm weary of hurting, weary of dragging myself through the same hoops I've jumped hundreds of times already. I feel betrayed—by my own behavior, by my community of faith. Everyone there seems to be doing fine. I almost believe they are. That hurts most of all. Mostly, I feel betrayed by God Himself."

Then the mask goes back on, the practiced smile returns and "seldom is heard a discouraging word, and the skies are not cloudy all day."

THOSE STILL SEARCHING FOR THE NEXT "NEW" TECHNIQUE

This group believes there's something preventing them from receiving what everyone else seems to have. They know their life isn't fine. They listen to message after message, podcast after podcast, growing more disillusioned that they'll ever get what others have.

> *"Just give me something I can add to my game plan to fix me without too much pain and change."*

But like dieters on their eleventh plan, we're growing increasingly skeptical. We throw baling wire over our issues, and we know it. There must be a new answer. There has to be. The God we trust wouldn't be playing with our heads... would He?

This twisted reasoning begins to creep into our thinking:

What's wrong with me? Nothing works. Maybe, after what I've done, I don't deserve answers. Others seem to figure this stuff out while I stay the same. Nothing is getting me to the abundant life I'm supposed to be experiencing.

We adopt formulas, strategies and disciplines promising to change us, but we remain ultimately the same. We know it, and we fear others are beginning to learn it, too. Maybe we've learned a new vocabulary and can rearrange the furniture on our behaviors, but deep inside, we're pretty sure we're only slightly different than we were. If others could spend a moment inside our heads, they'd be disgusted by what they'd discover. We can't imagine what we'd do if others learned the truth about us. So we pretend to know more than we do. We offer answers to others, knowing those answers aren't working for us.

We're starting to lose hope that we can change. We suspect that what we're missing is hidden from our ability to fix.

Some reading this are thinking, "Hey, people, get it together! What's wrong with you?" We may soon discover we are part of a third group.

THOSE WEARING THE PEDIGREED MASK

We're the "together" folk, the postcard family: well-educated, well-heeled, well-groomed, well-assured, well-positioned…and, well, a lot of work for everyone else.

Our lives don't really have all this messy stuff in it. We can't figure out why there are so many messed-up Christians. "What's the hang-up? Get over it."

We'd never say it, but it feels like we're superior, to some extent. We don't really need the help from God others do. We're deeply grateful for what He did on the cross but can't relate to words like "dependence," "needs," "vulnerability," and "unresolved issues." It's just not that hard for us. Our home and family and hobbies are almost as together as we are. Our lawns are immaculate. We don't need help or answers; we are help and answers. At least in our circles, we're the standard others are measuring themselves against. We don't need vulnerability. Vulnerability is for the needy. And needy doesn't keep your lawn immaculate.

We intimidate others. Honestly, we probably should. Most of them are jealous. If they had our self-determination and discipline, they wouldn't have to be intimidated. Their issue ultimately is not with us, but with not being able to live up to their own standard.

.   .   .

This group is the most maddening to the rest of us. They almost seem like they don't need God in their daily life. They are above such need, somehow.[8] Maybe the Gnostics were right after all. Maybe there really is a superior race of people who don't need God like the rest of us. "Self-managed maturity" is the best way to describe their lives. They don't pretend it's the superiority of their relationship with God that makes them so. There's just something innate that makes them great, and it's almost as if God should be thankful they're here.

They are deeply self-aware and comfortable in their own skin. They display maturity and self-control that those of us who depend on Jesus with our entire beings can't seem to harness. Because of their great confidence in their own ability and success, they have little motivation to place their trust in the grace or love of God. They've apparently learned how to live daily life without God. God is a peripheral element to their lives, like a hobby. Their faith makes them that much more rounded and healthy. They are aloof to a tender connection with Jesus and sense little need for Him except as the basis for their values and principles. Their only real concern that something might keep them from becoming the self-actualized "perfect" version of themselves.

This pedigreed group has probably put this book down already. Or they're reading it to better understand their messed-up Uncle Floyd. Ironically, this group may be the neediest, most desperate of all. Their masks are the hardest to remove because they have the most difficulty admitting their masks are there at all.

While this group's résumé and gentility are impressive, they're still man-made. The pride that put Christ on a cross dwells richly in this group. Their masks, though minimal and elegant, are the most dangerous form of mask. Even grotesque, disfiguring masks at least allow the wearer no doubt he's wearing one.

Here's another problem: Others can't relate. They don't know how to love those with pedigreed masks, how to receive love from them, how to trust. The pedigreed are admired and inspire imitation but are also veiled and unknowable. They are majestic, benevolent emperors—wearing no clothes at all.

With the exception of the last group, most of us will, if challenged, admit to wearing masks. We don't like our masks, necessarily, but we have no idea how to take them off. If the thought didn't scare us so much, we'd have shed them long ago, but most of us have no idea where they came from.

That's why revealing the origins of our masks is so important. We need to see ourselves objectively within our story, to see what drives the responses tripping us up. Our controlling behavior is rarely random. It's triggered by unresolved junk, and if we begin to understand the process of unresolved sin, we may no longer react to each new provocation like lemmings sprinting for the nearest cliff. Our masks are a symptom, not a root cause, a fever indicating a raging infection deep inside. We must expose this dark dynamic compelling us to protect ourselves.

OUR REAL PROBLEM

When we sin, or when someone else sins against us, we automatically respond. If we commit the sin, our automatic response is called guilt.[9] If someone sins against us, our automatic response is called hurt.[10] God graciously designed these two responses to signal that something wrong has happened, that our hearts are disrupted and need healing. We don't work at producing these two responses to sin. They're as natural as the sting we feel when we leave our hand over a flame too long.

Most of us don't know what to do with these internal responses, though. Like Adam, we feel naked, so we hide or override our guilt and hurt. In the moment, it seems like necessary self-preservation. But remaining in that choice soon unleashes new depths of pain, inner turmoil, and new masks to wear.

As with an undiagnosed infection spreading poison through our system, we may recognize something is not right. We don't have the energy we used to, and we wince and feel things we hadn't before. Still, we may not connect the dots. An invisible, inner enemy is draining our joy. We may ignore it or stuff it away, and it may lie dormant for a while, but unresolved sin is still there. Bacterial infections often keep spreading poison until antibiotics are introduced. You can dress nicer and comb your hair all you want, but you'll only be a well-dressed sick person with nicely combed hair. No external appearance or vigorous exercise will solve our infection. That is why we named this book The Cure.

Nothing in us is equipped or designed to absorb sin. Even when I'm the one being sinned against, I cannot handle it, because it will always ignite the nature of the sin already in me. So, I give myself permission to respond sinfully. How twisted is that? It makes me want to cry out, "It's not fair! I didn't start this. I wasn't the one who sinned!" It is not fair, but sin doesn't play by the rules.

The transformational good news is that the damage can stop at any time by trusting and applying God's power to resolve that sin.[11] If we don't access God's resources, the devastating pattern continues, and our guilt or hurt will then breed half a dozen more ugly responses. We call these inevitable effects: blame, fear, denial, anger, and their assorted sickly relatives. Something under our own roof begins to destroy us, and most of us are clueless about this chain reaction. We only know we have deep painful feelings, distorted, dysfunctional thoughts, and befuddling behaviors we feel the need to mask.

Among the damaging behaviors resulting from unresolved sin:

♦ We become highly sensitized to our own sin and judge the sin of others.
♦ We lose our objectivity in a crisis and become the issue.

26

- We hide our sinful behaviors and become vulnerable to more sin.
- We are unable to love or be loved.
- We become more susceptible to wrong life choices.
- We attempt to control others.

When we don't resolve our sin—either because we don't know how or choose not to—we release an inevitable force draining our confidence in who we really are.

The next thing we know, we're looking for a top-of-the-line mask, maybe several: "I'm better than most"; "I don't care"; "I'm self-sufficient"; "I'm important"; "I'm competent enough to be loved"; "I have answers others don't"; or "I'm independent." But all the while, our lies whisper, "You're an imposter. You always have been. You always will be. You may fool others, but I know who you are. You're an embarrassment. You have no credibility or self-respect. You spent it long ago."

It's expensive to wear a mask. First, no one—not even those I love—gets to see my face. There are moments when a hint of the real me bleeds through, but mostly I'm as confusing to others as I am to myself. Worse, I never experience the love of others because it's not the real me. So, I sense I'm still not loved and I self-diagnose. Maybe my mask wasn't tight enough, so then I continue searching for a better mask, convinced the next one will give me what I need, prove I'm worthy to receive love. I can't love behind a mask, at least not fully. Those I long to love experience only the cloying attempts of someone who doesn't really exist.

Many of us stopped on those last sentences and sighed at the realization we've wasted years of missed love and stunted maturity.

When we influence wearing a mask, we convince others:

- They too must live a two-faced life.
- They too must present an idealized person.
- They too must hide what is true about them.
- New life in Christ doesn't really work.
- They will remain stuck in their unresolved life issues.

♦   It is better to be unknown than to risk rejection.
♦   Self-protection is their only hope.

In the end, we're not just actors. We're also irrational directors of a badly over-stylized play, teaching those we love how to pose and masquerade, memorize fake lines, rehearse expressions, and produce false tears on command.

Our masks deceive us into believing we can hide our true selves. We can't. In time, others can usually see what we're trying to hide. No matter how beautifully formed, our masks eventually reveal us as warped figures. All masks eventually crack, buckle, or unravel.

So, why do believers wear more masks than others? All masks are the product of pretending something in our lives is true, even if experience denies it. We may even be fueled by a sincere desire to make God look good by having our act together. He has no need for such help, but we think it's our duty. So, we hide our scars and pretend we're modeling to the world how well God treats His followers. Instead, we just come off weird and smug.

The greatest hope for any mask-wearer is in understanding all masks eventually crack and dissolve, gradually revealing what is hidden beneath. All masks crumble because they are man-made.[12]

This is a good thing, though. Imagine if the mask didn't crack. It would forever separate us from love, authenticity, and freedom. We could go our entire lives missing what we were created to enjoy. Our endlessly loving God allows our masks to fall apart because He cares so deeply for us.

Once we weary enough of mask-wearing, we can begin rediscovering the true face of Jesus. He is the centerpiece in the Room of Grace. Jesus will always nudge us further out into the open, allowing our true faces to be revealed. Our true faces are beautiful, too. God made them exactly the way He wanted, and He longs to see His reflection.[13] The trouble with papier-mâché is, it doesn't reflect.

All of us wake up one day to the pain of realizing we can't control our lives the way we thought we could. We're still stuck with unresolved issues, symptoms we're trying to fix, without anyone's help.

Only that sort of revelation will free me into the stunning, life-giving hope of this next statement:

> *"What if there was a place so safe that the worst of me could be known, and I would discover that I would not be loved less but more in the telling of it?"*

That place exists. And when you reach it, unresolved issues will begin to heal. You'll gather up stacks of masks and toss them in the dumpster, brushing your hands together as you walk away. Then, you'll walk out into the daylight, your skin feeling the morning air for the first time since you can remember. You'll drink in the beauty of flowers and earth, free from those nauseating fumes of epoxy holding your face to a mask.

CHAPTER THREE | TWO GODS

*"You have as much God as you're gonna get! He lives in you!
You are in Him. How much closer do you want than that?"*

I left the Room of Grace last week. I didn't tell anyone. I just walked out.

I failed again. As much as I wanted to, when I needed it most, I couldn't handle Jesus' arm around me. The whole thing sounds so great until I screw up.

So, late one night, I slipped out and found my way back to the Room of Good Intentions. It's a long walk from the fork to either destination but there's a direct path between the Room of Grace and the Room of Good Intentions, so it actually isn't far at all. The path skirts the coastline, and it's gorgeous by night, but I didn't pay much attention. Soon the path wound back into the woods and the Room of Good Intentions loomed ahead over the trees. Soon enough, I broke into a clearing and there it was, the gleaming marble towering above me. The familiarity of it all immediately enveloped me, like an old hooded sweatshirt. I stood there, hands in pockets, for maybe an hour, staring at my sin. Though the heat off the mound of my garbage obscured me from seeing Jesus, I imagined Him, on the other side, shaking His head in disappointment. Disrupting His holiness with my selfishness felt...it's strange, I know, but it felt right. It felt like what I deserved.

I was jolted out of the moment by a voice behind me on the path. "You know, if you really want to sneak out, you're gonna need to shut the door more quietly."

I turned as the voice emerged from the shadows, and I was startled by his face. It was the loud guy with the chronic lower-back pain.

"You done here yet?"

"What do you mean?"

"I mean, let's get out of here. I'm not dressed for this crowd. I'm in my pajamas."

I could see that he was. "How did you know to find me here?"

"Where else would you go? I used to make the pilgrimage myself often enough."

"Really? I'm not the only who's done this?"

"Oh, it happens all the time. Soon as you walked out the door, someone yelled, 'We got a runner!' I figured it might be you. So I started walking. Look, you don't have to come back with me. Stay as long as you like. I just wanted to make sure you weren't beating yourself up."

"I was."

"I know."

Without a word, he turned and I followed.

After a while, back on the path winding toward the coast, I asked, "Why did I do that? Why did I come back here? That first day in the Room of Grace, I thought I'd never see life the same."[1]

"You don't see life the same. But the stories we tell ourselves can run deep. It's one thing to have a profound experience, and it's quite another to kill a lie that's served you a long time. Especially a lie you've used to cope. Until you see God right you'll keep going back there."

"What's that supposed to mean?"

"There are two gods: the one we see through our shame, and the One who actually is."

"Okay… I think I'm tracking here."

"So, think back to what you told me about Jesus with His arm around you. Did you believe it?"

"Yeah, I guess I'm starting to. But…" I trailed off.

"But what?" he asked.

"Well, when I pictured it later, His arm is around me, but He's not smiling. He's got this look of pity. There's no joy. It's like a friend comforting a dying patient, someone who's sick and never gets any better. And there's never anyone else around. He's disappointed in me. But He loves me enough to keep holding on. I know He won't leave me…I just didn't turn out like He hoped."

"Ah. My friend, you're still believing in the god your shame created, the god you've learned to fear."[2]

"This is all so hard to wrap my head around," I said. "Everything I've ever been taught—everything I've ever experienced—tells me you get what you put in. So, when I fail, it seems only right I should get less of God, which makes me want to be better. I want to put in more, so I'll get out more. Then I get down on myself when I take Him for granted or when I don't do right, or when I care about something more than Him. That seems like what He wants. If I were God, that's what I'd want out of people."[3]

He laughed. "That seems pretty self-righteous, doesn't it?"

"You're saying it's not?"

"Let me say it again: You have as much God as you're gonna get! He lives in you! You are in Him.[4] How much closer do you want than that? Every moment of every day, fused with you, there He is. He never moves,[5] never covers His ears when you sin, never puts up a newspaper, never turns His back. He's not over on the other side of your sin, waiting for you to get it together so you can finally be close. It's incredible! Don't you think? That's why they call it 'Good News'!"

"Then why doesn't it feel like it?" I blurted, then sighed to level myself. "I live with me. It feels like I'm playing a game of denial to believe He's not disappointed with me. I know He loves me, but where's the accountability to live this life for Him?"

The woods thin and clear, giving way to grassy dunes and eventually the sea. It was all lit up by the moon, nearly clear as day. I couldn't believe I didn't notice it earlier. My new friend looked at it all thoughtfully, like he was trying to find another way of explaining what I was missing. After a moment, he turned back.

"The goal is not to change me. I'm already changed.[6] The goal is to mature.[7] When I depend on the new creature I've been made into through the work of Jesus at the cross, I begin to live healthier, more free of sin, more free to love. I learn to believe all His power, love, truth, and goodness already exists in me, right now. Even on my worst day."[8]

"But if people believe this, won't they take advantage of God?"

"Yeah, I imagine they would," he responded. "Except they no longer want to do such a thing. They are new creations.[9] God lives in them to encourage, correct, and even rebuke. The reason people rebel is not because they trusted grace or chose to live out their new identity. It's the very opposite. It is moralism, the law of religious practice and thought, that keeps them trying to get away with something."

"Wow. I've never heard anyone say that."

"Look, Jesus says we really are new people, completely righteous. Jesus became sin so we might be righteous. Jesus didn't become theoretical sin. He actually became real sin, in every possible way that sin can be sin. And if the corollary holds, then we didn't become theoretical righteousness. We became real righteousness in every possible way that righteousness can be righteousness.[10] That didn't happen to anyone before Jesus.[11] Now we're free. But it isn't the freedom to get away with stuff, to give ourselves permission to have three glasses of wine instead of one. It isn't freedom to care less or walk the tightrope of right and wrong without remorse. The motive of a righteous heart is not to get away with anything. The motive of the righteous is to be loved and to love! That's what we've all been wanting for all of history. That's the freedom Jesus died for.[12] We can now love each other well, because it's who we really are."

Then it was silent for a while, just the waves and the moon and a soft wind. Then, when the horizon faded from blue black into purple and finally into orange as the sun peeked out over the waves, we walked again, together, all the way back to the Room of Grace.

.   .   .

YOUR VIEW OF YOU IS THE GREATEST COMMENTARY ON YOUR VIEW OF GOD.

Nothing you believe and depend upon is more magnificently freeing than this single truth: You are no longer who you were, even on your worst day. Trusting and leaning upon "Christ in you" is the source of every shred of strength, joy, healing, and peace.

—What we believe happened in that first moment of trusting Jesus affects everything. That start is called "justification," which means to be made right. Think about what it means to believe you were made right.

Some believe they will eventually, through sincere diligence, change into someone better. Their confidence to change centers on sanctified self-effort.

Others believe the very essence of who they now are is completely changed. They are convinced of absolute *fused union* with the God of the universe. Their confidence to mature is placed squarely in trust of their new identity in Jesus.[13] This does not mean they don't fail. They do fail. But in the end they trust who God has made them.

If I follow the first path, I'm trying to change from *who I was* into *who I should be*. If I follow the second, I'm maturing into *who I already am*.[14] In the first, I'm working toward becoming more righteous. In the second, I'm already righteous, made right by God in the moment I believed.

There were seasons early on when I believed:

♦   I have been changed into a new creature. I am fused with Jesus.
♦   He loves me and enjoys me all the time.
♦   He is maturing me in His way, in His time.
♦   I can trust and receive love.

Most of the rest of my time I've believed:

♦   I changed in a legal sense, but not really.
♦   He is usually disappointed with me.
♦   He expects me to at least try to fix myself.
♦   I can't be trusted or trust anyone else.

This is the cruel joke we play on ourselves: to bluff and pretend we are righteous, secretly knowing we aren't, only to eventually discover we actually were all along!

Much of our difficulty accepting this new life has to do with the *shame* we carry. Shame. It whispers and hisses that no matter what you do, you will always be defined by what you did or what was done to you. It mocks you. Shame wants you desperately performing for acceptance you don't believe you deserve.

That's when we begin to form the *fake* god. We imagine Him staring at us with a thin smile and a measured nod. He has to love us, but He's not sure He *likes* us. His arms are folded. He wears an expression that says, "Yes, your sins are forgiven. Your ticket's punched for eternity. But don't get lazy! You've got to stop being such a slug. And don't think I missed that last wrong thought you had four minutes ago. I'm not stupid. I still keep a list. I just don't lose my temper as much. What are you staring at? Get to work!"

How can we draw close to a god we imagine saying, "Sure, your sins are forgiven, but you're still the same failure. You had an excuse before, but not anymore."

WHAT DIFFERENCE DOES ANY OF THIS MAKE IN WHAT YOU AND I ARE FACING RIGHT NOW?

Let's consider one area many struggle with: sexual sin.

Almost every book on fighting sexual sin focuses on how we can react better at the moment of temptation. Thousands of tips and techniques are laid out to keep us from acting out. While helpful, these books miss the point: We didn't reach this moment randomly. We got *here* by gradually distorting our view of God *back there*.

Those prevention tools made sense until we allowed ourselves to entertain a thought that would eventually lead us into crisis. The moment those safeguards are needed, it's too late. We no longer want them to help. We are now way past wanting to do right. The problem is actually rooted far back when our course was fundamentally altered. The problem is our distorted picture of God.

That distortion is a pall over our eyes, keeping light out.

That distortion is there because we believe these five things about God:

1. God can't satisfy me as much as this sin.
2. I've always been this way. I don't believe I'm powerful enough to change that.
3. There is something fundamentally wrong with me.
4. I don't believe God has been fully good to me.
5. I'm going to feel like a failure anyway, so I might as well enjoy it!

These are the root beliefs behind the permission we give ourselves to fail.[15] They all are formed from picturing God separated from us.

At that point, it's only a matter of time, opportunity and our particular areas of vulnerability.

That's why this is a big deal.

Those in the Room of Grace are continually allowing God to work on removing the pall from their eyes. Light pours in, and they are in the process of being freed to live beyond preoccupation over their next failure.

Those in the Room of Good Intentions are rarely willing to confront those five statements. They're too busy covering their tracks and grinding it out against temptation. The great regret is, they know they've already given themselves permission to fail.

In fact, the insidious truth about sin is that fighting it only serves to heighten the anticipated pleasure.

If you ever want to truly connect with a family member or friend who has issues of repeated failure, reaching the root of those five distortions about God will help you resolve and heal sin issues exponentially better than techniques tailored to a moment, or prevention gimmicks that work just fine until you don't want them to. The fruit will be a lifetime of conversation, hope, protection, and healing.

If we see God through a veil of shame, we'll think the goal is to "fix" the behavior. Shame wants us constantly trying to prove we're not as bad as we imagine. In the Room of Grace, however, we're learning to believe we are no longer identified by shame. Our God doesn't see us that way,[16] and He doesn't need us to see ourselves that way. We're free to trust His delight and love even in the midst of our erratic, maturing behaviors. He wants us to learn dependence on Him instead of performance. We're learning to trust His power in us. The beauty is, we actually fail less in doing so.

OKAY. SO, HOW DO WE KNOW WHETHER OUR RELATIONSHIP IS WITH THE GOD WE SEE THROUGH OUR SHAME OR THE GOD WHO REALLY IS?

Well, probably I'd have to ask what shame looks like in a relationship:

- Do I measure my closeness to God by how little I'm sinning or by my trust that, to the exact extent the Father loves Jesus, Jesus loves me?
- Do I see myself primarily as a "saved sinner" or a "saint who still sins"?
- When I talk to God, do I spend more time rehearsing my failures or enjoying His presence?
- Am I drawn to severe authors and preachers who challenge me to "get serious about sin" or those who encourage me to trust this new identity in me?
- Am I drawn to messages telling me I haven't done enough or those that remind me who I am so that I'm free to live out this life God's given me?
- Do I believe that one day I may achieve being pleasing to God, or am I convinced I'm already fully changed and fully pleasing?
- Is my hard effort being spent preoccupied with sin or in expressing and receiving love from others?
- Do I trust disciplines to make me strong or grace to strengthen me?

- ◆ Do I believe that God is not interested in changing me because He already has?
- ◆ Do I read the Bible as "You ought. You should. Why can't you? When will you?" or as "You can. This is who you now are"?

IT MAY FEEL LIKE A GAMBLE TO YOU, BUT IT IS NO GAMBLE TO GOD.

God has shown all of His cards, revealing breathtaking protection. He says, in essence, "What if I tell them who they now are? What if I take away any element of fear? What if I tell them I will always love them? That I love them right now, as much as I love my only Son?

"What if I tell them there are no logs of past offenses, of how little they pray, or how often they've let me down? What if I tell them they are actually righteous, right now? What if I tell them I'm *crazy* about them? What if I tell them that, if I'm their Savior, they're going to heaven no matter what—it's a done deal? What if I tell them they have a new nature, that they are saints, not saved sinners? What if I tell them I actually live in them now, my love, power, and nature at their disposal?

"What if I tell them they don't have to put on masks? That they don't need to pretend we're close?

"What if they knew that, when they mess up, I'll never retaliate? What if they were convinced bad circumstances aren't my way of evening the score? What if they knew the basis of our friendship isn't how little they sin, but how much they allow me to love them? What if I tell them they can hurt my heart but I'll never hurt theirs? What if I tell them they can open their eyes when they pray and still go to heaven? What if I tell them there is no secret agenda, no trapdoor? What if I tell them it isn't about their self-effort, but about allowing me to live my life through them?"

Nature provides many examples of this incredible discrepancy between who we appear to be and who we truly are. Consider the caterpillar. If we brought a caterpillar to a biologist and asked him to analyze it and describe its DNA, he would tell us, "I know this looks like a caterpillar to you. But scientifically, according to every test, including DNA, this is fully and completely a butterfly." Wow! God has wired into a creature looking nothing like a butterfly a perfectly complete butterfly identity. And because the caterpillar is a butterfly in essence, it will one day display the behavior and attributes of a butterfly. The caterpillar matures into what is already true about it. In the meantime, berating the caterpillar for not being more like a butterfly is not only futile, it will probably hurt its tiny ears!

So it is with us. God has given us the DNA of righteousness. We are saints. Nothing we do will make us more righteous than we already are. Nothing we do will alter this reality. God knows our DNA. He knows that we are "Christ in me." And now He is asking us to join Him in what He knows is true!

THE BEST THING YOU COULD DO

It is hard to grasp how incredibly this would free our world, our children, our friends, our church, our neighborhood, our businesses, ourselves—everything—if we choose to believe it!

The best thing you could do at this moment is to put this book down, lace up your shoes, and take a long, slow walk through the neighborhood, and imagine. Imagine such a life.

Once you can imagine it, you can start to consider the risk and reward of it.

Once you can consider it, you can begin to believe it. Once you can believe it, you can begin to risk trying it out. Once you try it out, you can begin to enjoy it.

Once you can enjoy it, you will find others to join you. Once someone joins you, others will follow.

And once others follow…well, you get where this is going.

So, here we are, daring to risk believing that His arm is around us and He is not embarrassed or disgusted. Maybe I'm beginning to grasp the concept, for moments at a time, that I have, at this exact moment, all of God I'm ever going to get here on earth. And to enjoy it and avail myself of it, all I have to do is trust! We feel seditious and frightened to even imagine thinking such a thing. But there it is. And now the fun begins.

Well, out into the night air with you. We'll be here when you get back.

CHAPTER FOUR | TWO SOLUTIONS

"I stop believing God is able or good enough to solve my flaws."

I run into the hostess who welcomed me when I first arrived in the Room of Grace. I'm awkward at first. She's uncomfortably attractive, with the kindest voice. She asks how it's been for me, how I'm getting along in this new way of life. I tell her, "I can't believe I ever lived any other way. It saddens me it took so long to find this place. Sometimes, I'm angry nobody told me sooner."

I ask her the question haunting me: "You may know I went back to the old room last week. And even now, for moments, I think about going back. Why would I do that? Why would I consider going back to a place that nearly destroyed me?"

She pauses and breathes deeply for a moment before answering. "I wonder if it's because it rewards who we thought we needed to be."

"Huh?" My face contorts in confusion.

She pauses, like she's deciding whether she should make her next statement.

"What would you say if I told you I've gone back more than once?" She looks past me, then back. "Look, I'm late for a meeting right now. But I'd like to tell you more. It might help answer your question of what to do when you're drawn back. I'll bring my husband. He helps me tell the story. Coffee lounge? This time tomorrow?"

"I'd really like that."

And with that she's off.

The next day I'm sitting with the two of them at a corner booth in the coffee lounge off the Room of Grace's main hall. It's inviting here: the rich scents of roasted beans, the steaming cups. It's a

43

favorite place to gather, but it's not too busy today. The hostess introduces me to her husband, a quiet man with a broad smile and a contentedness about him. We spend some time getting to know each other. Then she moves to the reason we're here. "You were asking yesterday what could possibly make us consider going back to the Room of Good Intentions. It starts with the false stories we tell ourselves. We create lies about ourselves to make sense of the pain we suffered or the pain we caused."

"Everyone does this?"

"Everyone. Me, you, your grandma...everyone. These false stories become permission we grant ourselves to find meaning in something less than healthy relationships. Permission to fail. Permission to succeed at all costs. Either way, we're just waiting, helpless, for an opportunity to fail. Does that make sense?"

"Sorta."

"Let me ask you this: Do you ever picture God 'over there'? By that, I mean do you ever picture Him on the other side of your sin, and the sin is like a chasm or mountain between you?"

I sit back, stunned for a moment. "Yeah! That started dawning on me just last week!"

"It's very common, seeing God that way. That's how it starts with me. I see a picture of God 'over there,' indignant and aloof to my heart and my needs, hurts, failures...the wrong that has happened to me. Then I start trying to solve the hurt by myself, but I don't even know the base issues, let alone how to fix them! But that's what I do. I stop believing God is able or good enough to solve my flaws.

"Then I feel sorry for myself, like I'm a victim of God's random acts and lack of protection. This is where the self-entitlement comes in: 'I deserve this. I owe this to myself. God doesn't understand me or my needs. I don't think He cares fully and He's been holding out on me.'

"And now my heart's inflamed, hooked, ready to plot a move."

I replay a dozen times I've experienced that very series in my head as she speaks. "I've known that sequence of events all my life. I've never been able to break it."

"Yes. The Room of Good Intentions ignores that entire rebellious system of permission. It only pays attention to the acting out. That's why most of the books on addiction and overcoming sin only address the techniques to fight the moment of temptation. By that point, though, the game is already over."

"I've got a dozen of those books," I say.

Her husband laughs. "Me, too. I think I kept that literary genre alive single-handedly."

"So, my story is about an absent dad," she continues. "I guess I never felt like I was valuable enough for him to change his schedule.

"He's still alive and we've walked through a lot of what I'm telling you. But back then, he didn't know how to express love. He was trying so hard to become someone, to make his mark. He didn't have much meaningful time for an overweight, clumsy little girl with braces. A daughter is built to adore her dad, but not all dads realize this completely. He was successful in anything he tried. Competition was his lifeblood. His praise for me was always measured and usually followed by correction or comparison. The only real affirmation I got was when I achieved something public, but that rarely happened. The message was clear: Who I was wasn't quite enough.

"So that story ran around my head all day, every day, as I grew up. Until I decided to make myself enough. I mean, who can live in a world where you aren't worth your father's affection? You start to find ways to prove you are enough, because maybe then someone will notice you and you will be loved."

Tears form in her eyes.

"So, an awkward little girl quietly and deliberately transforms herself into a presentable young woman. She learns to dress just right, learns to communicate cleverly and say important things at important parties. She grows out of her oafishness and becomes quite athletic. She feverishly works on her weight until she becomes attractive. She marries a very competent, emotionally guarded man, much like her dad. From her hairstyle to her clothes to how she dresses her kids, she has it together."

"'Competent' and 'emotionally guarded,'" he laughs. "That was my default, all right."

"Do you see the cycle forming? This God-loving young woman, carrying around suitcases of unresolved junk and a dishonest self-story, experiences a fresh series of thoughts.[1] She's awakened, aware of her vulnerability. Soon, a familiar sin, a uniquely familiar offer of wrong pleasure, is presenting itself as an option."

"What does that look like?" I ask.

"Well, for me, it became conquest. It wasn't sexual, necessarily. I wanted to prove I was worth something. I began using my competency, intelligence, and looks to draw competent, intelligent, attractive men. I wanted them to be willing to risk something on me. That's all. I just needed to know that if I wanted to proceed further, they would go along. That's my vulnerability. An opportunity to prove I'm enough, by capturing the attention of another. It's a subtle game. I almost don't know I'm doing it at times. But it follows a predictable course, a predictable pattern.

"Without the self-story I created, I might leave it alone, trusting God's life for me. But the lie, the story of me not being enough, it's like rocket fuel. Now the story speeds up. Here's where it gets ugly. Somewhere in this whole blur, I give myself permission to act out. Maybe I send a vaguely flirtatious e-mail, or invite someone to ask for my number. If questioned, I'd have to admit it is conscious on some level, but I hide it from myself. Yet, I do give myself permission. Thankfully, I never took it much further than that, but if I had continued to live in the lie of my self-story, it was just a matter of time and opportunity until I carried this out."

Sitting there, listening to this couple willing to tell me this story, reminds me how beautiful and strong this room is. Who tells on themselves like this? Who is this honest? Her husband isn't smiling now, but he is fully supportive, placing a gentle hand on her shoulder. She gives him a thankful look.

"So, this awareness of vulnerability, allowed space, is now given an opportunity. It explodes into full-blown temptation. No longer just theoretical vulnerability, it now has a name, a time, a location, and a real possibility for something to happen."

She presses on, even as it's clear this is painful for her. She's almost unwilling to come up for air until she gets this all out. "The Room of Good Intentions gives you only one tool to deal with this onslaught: resistance. It seems to make sense, after all. I know what I'm considering is wrong. I know I should fight it, even if I don't want to abandon it. Even if it never goes any further than a veiled e-mail exchange, I still know this is not who I want to be. That's the vulnerability. For me, with my story, that's where I go. Everyone is different.

"So, I resist it for a while. 'I'll talk myself out of this; I'll resist enough; I'll stuff it away.' That's the problem with sin-management. It treats sin lightly, as if I could control it. Grace is not soft on sin. Attempting to manage my sin is."

She looks up, "Want to know the worst part about my attempted resistance?"

Only half joking, I respond, "I'm not sure."

"It's not the sin I'm obsessed with. It's the promised pleasure of the sin.[2] That elation, that euphoria I'm hoping will come with the conquest. Remember? That's the part they don't tell you about resistance in the Room of Good Intentions. The extended resistance actually heightens the promised pleasure of my eventual acting out. The longer and more intense the battle, the bigger the payoff when I finally cave.

"So I hide my temptation from others, knowing my resistance is not going to be enough to stop. Eventually, I become aware I'm going to act out. I no longer pretend I'm not fully bought in. To act out, though, I have to go into hiding,[3] where I can start plotting the event. I don't go away literally, but I may as well. My kids, my husband, my friends, will now no longer receive my focus and devotion. I'm preoccupied in isolation, trying to figure out the next steps and planning how I'll manage the consequences afterward. And sitting alone, hidden, I find a strange comfort in the sin I'm intending."

I don't need clarification on any of this. The details are different, but she's describing the cycle of my sin as clear as glacier water.

"Eventually, I act out. Sometimes this cycle takes a month; sometimes it happens in the course of a lunch, with someone several tables away. It truly does deliver the pleasure it promised. It always does, or I wouldn't risk it. It could be one line in an e-mail hinting he'd be willing to take this further. Sometimes it's just grabbing an undeniable look from across a room. Whatever form it takes, it serves the purpose. I've compromised who I am; I've given in to what I know is wrong. I've betrayed my husband and created another life I can never expose to my family. Tragically, the more often I play this out, the greater loss of intimacy I create in my real world.

"In this trap, I deceive myself into thinking I can manage the consequences of the choice.[4] What delusion! I couldn't even manage the events leading up to the failure! How am I supposed to manage the consequences? I withdraw from my most important relationships—the ones who love and need me the most. I can't let anyone too close for fear I'll slip or my betrayal will show on my face. In my withdrawal, I'm monitoring an ongoing ticker with periodic assessments of damage control. At this point, it's exhausting."

Her husband puts his hand on his wife's. He says, "I know her so well now, I can tell when she's in this place. For a long time, I just didn't want to admit it. We'd be watching a movie or listening to a friend tell an anecdote, and she'd miss the punch line. Everyone in the room is smiling and laughing, and my otherwise brilliant, clever wife is somewhere else entirely."

"It doesn't stop here," she steps in. "It is so hard to live in guilt, so hard to face the reality of what I know I'm capable of, that it's much easier to justify my actions. 'It didn't really hurt anyone. No one needs to know.'

"This inevitably leads to blame.[5] Someone else must be held accountable for my choice. So I rehearse how my needs have not been taken care of, or how I have not been loved well. I become the judge and jury of others' behaviors."

He adds, "This stage is predictable, too. I just couldn't always tie it together. One day she's reasonable and thoughtful. The next, she's a particularly aggressive traffic cop. Suddenly, I can't do enough. Or whatever I'm doing is wrong. I'm walking on eggshells, trying to not get on her bad side. Some of our worst fights were born in this part of the cycle. Blame is often a commentary on the unresolved, hidden sin in the blamer."[6]

She nods. "Maybe the worst aspect of this whole cycle is that it reinforces the shame that got me into the mess in the first place. This failure adds another layer. 'Well, my dad was right. I'm not enough. Something's uniquely wrong with me. Who would keep doing such a thing?' So I spend a season in awareness of my shame, another chapter in the false self-story I tell myself. I don't realize that only grace through love can overcome my shame. And, I cannot experience this love unless I trust others with me.

"Inevitably, I begin to lose hope. I cannot be trusted. I cannot trust myself. I want to trust no one. I begin to doubt my life in Christ has even made a difference. My track record shows I've always been this way and always will be. I don't like being me; I don't like my own companionship. I find myself saying, 'I don't care anymore.' It's an ugly place to dwell.[7]

"For a while, the realization of my lost hope makes me so disgusted with my behavior, I don't struggle so much. Maybe this last episode got my attention. Maybe I'm growing up. Maybe this period of time with no temptation and no acting out is proof I'm gaining control of this sin after all! But this, too, is self-delusion. Another opportunity, another awareness, another expression of my false story is right down the road. It is served best when I believe I'm getting better." She stops speaking. None of us is saying anything. It's like we've just watched a violent car wreck in slow motion.

Finally, she looks straight into my eyes.

"That is why we would go back to a room that almost destroyed us."

I realize I'm afraid. Afraid maybe I'll never get better. Afraid I'll always leave this place because I'll always fail too much to feel right staying here. "So, where's the hope against this cycle we have no power to overcome? There's gotta be hope. Right?"

They both smile.

"Oh, there is great hope, my friend," she says softly. "This cycle will never go away. Not completely. Even after years in this room. But this room gives me, gives you, a chance to stop the cycle that the other room can never offer. Amidst our healing, our maturing, our learning to love, there is a great gift that can help us stop this cycle at any point."

"So?" I ask, searching their faces.

"So," she says kindly, with the same smile she gave me the moment I met her in this place. "I've got to watch the front entrance for a while. Shall we all continue this discussion over dinner?"

.   .   .

THE CONTROL CYCLE

We've just ridden a journey through the control cycle. We call it that because it is what happens when we believe we can control our lives. And control our sin.

We watched an inevitably tightening cyclone of increasing despair:

- Building defenses
- Thinking unhealthy self-thoughts (shame-driven lies)
- Being tempted
- Trying to resist sin
- Hiding secrets
- Acting out
- Withdrawing from others
- Justifying behavior
- Blaming people and circumstances
- Feeling shame
- Losing hope

These are the order of sin.
This cycle reveals the nature of sin:[8]

- Sin always delivers its promised pleasure.
- I will become addicted to its pleasure.
- The addiction to this pleasure is incredibly destructive.
- The result is—in one form or another—death.

This cycle also reveals many realities about the nature of sin in me:

- Whenever I think I'm in control of sin, it is, in fact, controlling me.
- The power of sin is not when I act out. It's when I give myself permission.

- This is not simply a choice to act on temptation. It is a choice to dishonor God. I am saying, "God, I know this is wrong and I'm going to do it anyway. And You can't stop me because I'm in control."
- Once I choose to hide, or go it alone, I have also decided I will use someone to satisfy my sin.[9]
- All unresolved sin issues are buried alive in me.
- Addictive behaviors are not limited to pornography or drug dependence. Apart from medical and physiological issues, they can express themselves in mood swings, depression, substance abuse, lying, spending, unhealthy attention-seeking, anger, manipulation, gambling, unforgiveness, unrepentance, gossip…the list is long.
- If, at any stage of this cycle, I choose not to disclose, the next step is inevitable.
- My unhealthy self-thoughts (lies) fuel the entire cycle.
- If I don't trust you, you can't love me, no matter how much love you have for me.

That's the painfully bad news about the nature of sin. But there's good news too. For those in the Room of Grace, there's a way to stop the cycle.

YOU CAN TELL ANOTHER.

You can tell another what is going on inside before it happens. And the moment you tell with the motive of giving up control, the cycle can stop. Light shines on the madness, the rationalization, the pain, and the damage—and it can stop.

Please read this again.

The control cycle can be broken when we choose to tell.

You may need to break the cycle several times on a given day, but the power to break the cycle is no less. In fact, choosing to tell each time the cycle repeats can teach us to depend and trust on God and others' love that much more.

Once I understand how God sees me and who I am in Him, I can then:

- ◆ Learn to confess the sin I intend to commit rather than confessing the sin I've carried out, with all the consequences it brings. This is living in the light. My identity in Christ allows me to see the truth without having to hide in fear that failure will define me or confirm I'm not enough.[10]
- ◆ Tell someone in the first moment I recognize my vulnerability. Now, here's incredible beauty: We can only be loved when another is allowed to meet our needs. God created us with limitations so that we can be loved by others. Instead of pretending we're "doing fine," we give others an opportunity to love us. We experience their love as we learn to tell each other we're vulnerable.[11]

In the Room of Good Intentions, we must hide. The reality of the sin we're capable of tells us we are who our shame has declared us to be. In the Room of Grace, sin has no such power. I am "Christ in me" on my worst day, in my worst thought, during my worst temptation. So, I learn to tell on myself, both to God and to others. I experience the truth that living in holiness is living with nothing hidden. Then I am clean; I am free; I am healing. We are able to give our lives away when we are no longer preoccupied with failure. This is life indeed.

CHAPTER FIVE | TWO HEALINGS

"What if repentance wasn't a promise from you to God but a gift from God to you?"

It's one thing for people to spread lies and gossip back in the Room of Good Intentions. That's happened for as long as I can remember.

But if it can happen here, where people are supposedly products of grace, well, then is it really any different than where I came from?

Well, the one thing I never thought would happen around here did happen. I got hurt—really hurt—by another here in the Room of Grace.

I've spent almost the entire time alone the last few days, rehearsing this whole event. I'm embarrassed, angry, and afraid of what is probably being said about me. I feel horribly alone. The worst I've felt since I got here.

This morning I'm sitting alone in the corner of the coffee lounge, taking solace in an immaculately prepared cappuccino. I've got a book in front of me, but I'm finding it difficult to concentrate. Lively conversations are as thick as the scent of roasted beans. Of all people, the hostess's husband spots me as he pours his cream, and walks up to ask how I'm doing. Maybe he's unaware of the conflict. "How long you got?" I ask, motioning to the plush chair across from me. I tell him I'm angry and I feel betrayed. His nod is permission for me to unload. Without more than three breaths, I tell him everything…who hurt me, how I was hurt, the injustice, how it feels like everyone is siding with the offender. I tell him I am right.

Everything.

When I finish, he says nothing. He just sits there, still nodding. "Well? You're not going to say anything? I pour out all that and you got nothing?"

He stays completely quiet for about twenty seconds. Finally, he says, "Look, the whole thing sounds awful. I'm sorry you've had to go through it. But you're probably not going to hear whatever else I say to you right now. That's why it's taking me so long to respond."

I jump on his response. "You agree with them then? You think I'm wrong?"

"I didn't say that. Listen, this isn't going to make much sense right now, and you may want to lump me in with whoever you imagine is siding with the person who hurt you. But here goes: Whatever the specifics, you're going to have to forgive him before you have a chance at getting this thing right."

"You're kidding me. You gotta be kidding me! That's your response to what's been done to me? What about him?" I'm almost yelling now. "This is not on me! Excuse me."

I stand up in a hurry, bumping the table and knocking over my mug. It shatters against the tile floor, sloshing foam and espresso everywhere. "No, don't bother," I say, loud enough for everyone in the coffee shop to hear. "I'll get that. That was my fault, too. Like everything else. Right?"

.   .   .

If you haven't been here yet, you will. You'll be wronged, hurt, then feel left for dead in an environment promoting just the opposite. It's a dangerous moment, because it causes us to wonder whether a place of safety, authenticity, grace, and love is actually possible this side of heaven. It's here that many of us make the choice to return to our self-preserving ways. Many of the folks scattered and dazed along the road in chapter one reached that point in shock with no clue of what to do when betrayal and violation hit.

You know the pattern, right?

First, you get hurt. It's especially painful when the person hurting you is someone you care about. They intentionally do something to wrong you. Maybe they're willing to put your integrity in question to defend their position. They refuse to own it, or when challenged, they blame it back onto you.

You make sincere attempts to reconcile, to own your stuff. But it just gets more tense and strained. Soon you discover they're coughing their justification to an ever-growing audience, with supposedly dear friends now buying the other's version of the story.

Soon, you're increasingly alienated in your pain, forced to defend yourself against lies. God's silence makes you begin to wonder if He too has been poisoned by these false accusations!

Suddenly, in a fight you never wanted, you discover you're not only the victim but the issue.[1]

. . .

YOU BECOME PREOCCUPIED WITH THE EVENT.

You rehearse it over and over. You don't sleep well. Worse, you're devastated to discover the person who hurt you seems to be enjoying his life just fine, barely even able to remember the particulars of the event.

YOU BECOME A PROSECUTING ATTORNEY, CONSISTENTLY BUILDING YOUR CASE.

You now globalize accusations, often totally unrelated to the issue. You begin to rewrite the history of your relationship, repainting each memory into more proof that perhaps he might be a serial killer after all! Accumulated evidence mounts so high that you cannot possibly imagine any wrongdoing on your side. You forget that just because you're hurt, that doesn't mean you're right in every turn of the relationship.

YOU BECOME OBSESSED WITH "JUSTICE AND ACCURACY."

"Yes, but you said...!" You now have all the grace and flexibility of a warden. You judge motives, memorize exact words, demand payment, call for swift and severe sentencing.

YOU BECOME UNABLE TO LOVE WELL, NEGLECTING THE NEEDS OF OTHERS.

You're so preoccupied with your self-defense that you become largely aloof to the normally clear indications of others who need your attention, care and presence. You innately sense that you should protect your children from this issue, but are also no longer able to spontaneously drop into their worlds to playfully enjoy them. They gradually learn to do their daily lives without you. They aren't even sure what happened. They just miss you and are not sure how to tell you.

YOU BECOME UNABLE TO SEE FROM ANY OTHER VANTAGE POINT BUT YOUR OWN.

Your desperate need to hear the other's groveling repentance makes you rigid against seeing possible other motivations causing this event. Whatever wrong you may have done since then can be deflected as logical necessity from this incredible injustice.

YOU BECOME MORE AND MORE UPTIGHT AND YOUR JOY IS ROBBED.

Until justice happens, the judge, attorneys, jury, bailiff and stenographers are not allowed to go home. Between the incessant rehearsing of your side of the story and your vigilant gathering of evidence, you're about as fun as a clerk at the DMV.

YOU BECOME PROGRESSIVELY MORE UNHEALTHY.

Growing bitterness is causing you to become irrational, overbearing, hyper-sensitive, angry, and petty. It is hard even for friends to be around you for extended periods. You're not a safe person.

YOU BECOME INTENT ON TELLING "YOUR SIDE OF THINGS" TO AS MANY AS POSSIBLE.

Eventually, almost everyone you know is poisoned with your distorted, thinly veiled character assassinations.

YOU BECOME UNABLE TO INTERPRET HISTORY ACCURATELY.

Though you can quote statements perfectly that defend your case, your recall of what actually happened is becoming hazy. Your propaganda has polluted your own memory.

YOU GRADUALLY ALIENATE YOURSELF FROM ALL UNWILLING TO CARRY YOUR BANNER.

You demand that others take your side and be willing to get involved at some level. Unwillingness to do so brings friendship and loyalty into question.

YOU BECOME WILLING TO QUESTION GOD'S MOTIVES, INTENTIONS AND CARE.

This is the most heartbreaking and self-degrading result of your state. If God was for you,[2] if God could see better, if God was more concerned about the truth—He'd do something on your behalf by now! The only conclusion you can eventually draw is that He's defending the case of your enemy. "Fine. You'll see you were wrong! I'll fight this by myself." Worship is bluffed, at best. You don't speak to God much now, except to bark out questioning of His actions.

In the Old and New Testament, writers expressed repeatedly that God has to stand against the proud but loves giving grace to the humble.[3] We can almost picture God forced to sit on His hands, waiting until we give up so He can rescue us. This is the collateral damage of our choice to refuse His gift of forgiveness. We become proud. The pattern laid out above is simply a person's pride being revealed. If humility is "trusting God and others with me,"[4] then the proud are those who are untrustingly self-protective. God works to speed us to a place of humility, where we can be freed from our self-obsessed deathtrap. This chapter is called "Two Healings." Its intent is to provide a way home and offer freedom from unforgiveness. The other "healing," the one we're tempted to believe, isn't healing at all. It is the result of white-knuckling our way to forgiveness through reciting the right words with no change of heart. We don't trust that healing at all. We know God wants us to forgive. What we can't figure out is why we can only do it superficially, or why we reject it alltogether as a hypocritical gesture, when the other hasn't repented.

The goal of this chapter is to give us a way of seeing forgiveness, releasing us from being judge and jury, from being the relentless detectives rooting out clues and holes in stories. Nothing is more wearying than refusing to forgive.[5]

If I'm to be set free, I must first embrace a forgiveness that is solely for my benefit. Only then can I extend forgiveness to the benefit of another. Until we understand the distinction, we can only conjure an external expression of forgiveness. Inside, we'll remain seething, our hurt and thirst for revenge buried alive.

The way home is not the expected route. I assume life will be right when everyone apologizes long enough and completely enough to me, in public, perhaps through a televised worldwide event. Justice will be served when I am vindicated, proven right, publicly honored, and all damaging consequences are rectified (with sufficient amends for emotional damage).

While God may actually do some of these things once we loosen our grip, that route home will never truly free us or give us what we hunger for. That route takes us deep into the desert, with no water.

The first condition to returning home is that we must be weary enough. We must be weakened to the point we drop our defenses long enough to look to God and call out, "Help!" This condition is called repentance. Now, you may be saying, "What? Repentance? Are you kidding me? I didn't do anything. I'm the victim, remember?" But remember the tragedy of not trusting forgiveness? You've carried bitterness and have chosen to ignore God's protection and go it alone. And often, in the subjectivity of your inflamed and wounded bitterness, you become blinded to your part in the issue. Your hurt has given you permission to absolve yourself of all wrongdoing. Repentance is God's antidote to the guilt you feel for both of these wrongs.[6] You must face, maybe with the help of a trusted other, the brutal honesty of an accurate assessment of your role in this.

It's important to remember that this repentance is not the "man-up" religious bluffing we've tried before. Repentance isn't doing something about my sin. It is admitting I can't do anything about my sin. It is trusting that only God can cleanse me, and only He can convince me I'm truly cleansed.[7]

We've been told repentance is a promise to God that *I'm going to stop this sin* and *I'm sorry* and *I won't do it again* and *This time I mean it.*

We're mistaking repentance for remorse. *The intention not to sin is not the same as the power not to sin.*

WHAT IF REPENTANCE WASN'T A PROMISE FROM YOU TO GOD BUT A GIFT FROM GOD TO YOU?

Paul calls repentance a gift.[8] It's not something you drum up, but the gifted ability to find yourself saying, "God, I can't. You can. I trust You!" "God, I am trusting what You did for me on that cross to cleanse me of what I've done." This is called redemption: *to liberate by payment, to release from debt or blame.*

Sin is resolved when we are cleansed of it. No amount of promises, amends, or right behavior can cleanse us. We are cleansed when we depend on the power of what Jesus did for us on the cross.[9]

Take a deep breath and look how far we've traveled. We're past the checkpoint of repentance. We've given the password that lets us through: "humility." That means trusting that God is with us, trusting God is for us, absolutely and completely able, never making any mistakes in moving us forward. He is fully sovereign. He loves me more than I love myself, and absolutely nothing can damage His total and complete control! He never messes up when it comes to you and me. I trust that even the worst events this life can bring are being used by God, forged into good, not religious, pretend good. Right about here, at this place in the road, many of us have been told that, because of what Jesus did for us, we should just let go of our rights, stuff our feelings, and get back to living for God. Such theology would have to improve to reach heresy.

God never tells me to get over something and just get past it. Never. Instead, He asks me to trust Him with every circumstance.[10] This involves communicating with Him honestly, in detail, until I'm sure I've left nothing out. He wants to hear it all. He wants to enter into every tear, every detail. He's been waiting for this moment. He's watched me go it alone. Now He will sit, elbows on knees, hands on chin, listening to every single word. I must sigh, cry, shriek, or howl, until He's certain I'm done, that I've gotten it all out.

There's no formula for the rest of the scene, but those of us who have gone before can suggest what it might look like. Are you ready? Many look at this section and turn away, afraid to feel the pain again. It may be valuable to have a trusted, safe friend walk you through this. At the other end are light and freedom and healing and beauty and safety and buttermilk donuts. (Note: Donuts don't actually come with the process. You have to go out and buy them. But it never hurts to have them nearby.)

THE ORDER OF FORGIVENESS

I Have to Admit Something Happened.

God's provision for my healing always begins with my recognition that someone has sinned against me. I may want to skip this step for a variety of reasons. If I was sinned against as a child—abused, neglected or demeaned—I may not even remember or realize what happened.

Or I may fear losing control of the relationship if I admit my hurt. I think if I don't admit my pain, no one will have control over me. Someone more articulate or powerful will not be able to manipulate me into believing I'm the guilty party.

Or I may want to deny that I have been hurt as a sign of my spiritual maturity: "This shouldn't bother me. I'll just move on."[11]

But I cannot forgive until I admit I've been sinned against. This is an invitation to stop hiding the sin someone else has committed against me. To forgive, I must admit what is already true.

I Must Get in Touch with the Consequences of My Act Done Against Me.

The consequences of sin are usually worse—sometimes far worse—than the sin itself. In order to understand the effect a sin has on me, I need to connect with how that event is impacting my daily life. Have I experienced shame? Have I become fearful? Have I felt demeaned or devalued? Was I manipulated or shunned? Were there relational effects? Did I lose credibility or access with friends? Was my marriage affected? Did it impact my relationship with my children or people I work with? Did it affect my job, my income, or my future? Did I lose my position or influence? Has this changed how I see myself or my attitude towards love, trust, friendship…God?

This is hard work. To understand the consequences of the sin, I have to allow myself to feel the pain of my responses. This work is sacred, though. Harboring enables the sin that was committed against me to define me! No more. Remember, unresolved sins are buried alive, even the ones carried out against us. We must take our time. God is there, nodding and smiling at the courage coming from our trust in Him. This hard work prepares us to forgive.

I Must Tell God What Happened to Me.

Now it's time to pour out my heart, telling Him, as best I can, exactly what has happened to me.

My old programming tells me He doesn't want to hear it. I might think, *No way! This is for over-emotional people. I don't do that stuff.* I might think any rehearsal of the event is akin to wallowing in it. I am wrong.

I might cry, scream, run around the room, or drive out into the desert and howl like a coyote—whatever feels right—but I must excavate every effect and emotion I've buried about the sin against me. Every last bit. This is the mysterious, beautiful part of my interaction with God. It is reclaiming this truth of our relationship: "You care even more deeply and fully than I do. Enter into this." For the first time in a long time, I feel heard, known, validated, and safe.

I Must Forgive the Offender, for My Benefit.

Wait…for *my* benefit?

Yes.

This section describes the missing piece in why forgiveness has not taken root in many of us. This is one of the most freeing, healing, practical expressions of God's power we can experience this side of heaven. God frees our hearts, eventually leading us to free the ones who've hurt us, and that process is central to God's deepest will and intentions.

Forgiveness has an order. We must initiate the *vertical transaction* with God before we can move into the *horizontal transaction* with another. First, before God, I forgive the offender(s) for what they've done and the consequences they've borne in my life. This is before God and me, and it is for *my* sake. It does not let anyone off the hook; it does not excuse any action. It does not restore relational forgiveness to the other. This is the vertical transaction. It is a choice to free myself, to begin healing.

Trusting God's character, strength, love and protection, I place the entire list of consequences and loss into His hands. This is a big decision. It's a scary, beautiful, overwhelming moment of trust.

I actually imagine removing every effect of that sin and placing it onto God. I hand over everything. I trust God will not mock me, or ignore this, or forget my pain. I trust He will protect me and defend my heart, bringing beauty out of hurt. I trust He will cleanse me as He promised.

I am giving up my rights to decide what is best for that person or myself. I'm handing the case over to the only Judge who can see the entire story and who loves both the offender and the victim perfectly. This is a unique moment when faith becomes a risked action. I'm putting everything on the line, because, after all, this is *my* life, *my* pain, *my* reputation. Never is the proof of new life more evident than when I cede control because of my trust in His character, love, and power. Then the whole incident moves out of my sphere and into God's.

Only then will I be freed to go to my offender and forgive him. If I don't get this right—if I attempt to forgive, unclean before God—I move toward my offender in veiled bitterness, judgment, and a spirit of retribution. I bring the residue of unresolved sin into the equation, and everyone can smell it.

If I say, "I'm not going to forgive until he repents," I end up in resentment. In my unwillingness to forgive before God, I become the issue.

The question then is, how do I know I've actually forgiven someone who's sinned against me? Answer: the moment I can offer that person my love again. When forgiveness stays only in my mind, as a formula or technique, it doesn't sink deep into my heart.

When I choose to let go, to forgive vertically before God, it's like huge cement bags have been lifted off my shoulders. It's like coming out of a moldy basement with a cement floor and suddenly breathing ocean air on the sand at Big Sur. It feels like being home.

And now, I'm ready to move on.

I Tell the Offender I've Forgiven Him When He Repents, for His Sake.

To declare "I forgive you" before a person has the opportunity to repent robs the offender of the opportunity for his own life-freeing repentance. God uses repentance to heal guilty hearts, and premature forgiveness will not free the other person from his offense or heal our relationship. The one who sinned against me must repent for his sake to be healed from that sin.

This is not a smooth or exact interaction. It can take many conversations, over a long period of time, to restore a relationship in truth and beauty. But there may not be a stronger, healthier, and more faithful relationship than one restored through repentance.

I can pursue reconciliation, but I can't force it. I can't demand repentance. Repentance requires trusting God's work. Insistence and $3.50 will get me a small latte and nothing more.

If my offender repents, I forgive with the goal of restoring the relationship, not just resolving a conflict. I desire his repentance, not to hold it over him, but so we can move on in mutual trust and love. His repentance will not heal my heart. That healing began when I forgave him before God. His repentance will begin to heal our relationship. As I forgive my offender for his sake, it prepares the way for the relationship to be restored.

Isn't that incredible? When I allow God to heal me from being sinned against, I get to turn around and help those who've sinned against me in healing their sin. It's just a beautiful process.[12]

I Must Distinguish Between Forgiving and Trusting My Offender.

Forgiveness is not a renewed demand that I now fully trust the other person. This misunderstanding causes many of us to balk at forgiveness. Because I can't trust a person, I believe I can't forgive him. Forgiveness and trust are separate issues. Even if I've forgiven my offender—even if my offender has repented and asked for forgiveness—I will still, in the future, have to deal with the issue of mutual trust. My expectations must be realistic, because while trust is easily broken, it is recovered very slowly. Sometimes it never recovers. Forgiveness carries the hope of renewed trust, but it offers no mandate or guarantee. Once I've risked baring my throat in pursuing forgiveness, trust longs to follow. From here, it is a matter of time, opportunity, and an open heart.

I Must Seek Reconciliation, Not Just Conflict Resolution.

Many of us, in our shame and self-protection, want to get past the issue and leave the relationship to die. Our effort will be to *resolve a conflict* rather than *reconcile a relationship.* That way, I imagine I can get past the ugliness and pain in my heart without letting go of my disdain and rigid resentment toward the other. This seems honorable, but the difference between resolution and reconciliation is like the difference between brussel sprouts and chocolate cake

When I give the other an opportunity to ask, "Will you forgive me?" I give the gift of engaging in the relationship. Repentance and forgiveness are not a means to fix our behavior. They are gifts of grace to heal our relationships. Reconciliation belongs in a completely different stratosphere than mere conflict resolution. When I want to "fix" a conflict, I will use terms like, "I'm sorry that happened," or "I really made a big mistake on that one." When I'm willing to say, "Will you forgive me because I did _____?" I create an opportunity for the other person to forgive me and enter back into a heart relationship with me.

In my eagerness to fix conflicts, I often push people to apologize. But no one stays "fixed" when I force the issue. I can say "I'm sorry," but sometimes those are just words. Nothing has been reconciled. We're left each defending our turf, still just as resentful, even if the "right" words have been spoken.

Grace always invites rather than demands reconciliation. An apology may push the issue away for the moment, but it won't heal a relationship, and it rarely solves any issue.

The courage to refuse quick fixes and to engage long and vulnerably enough to woo honest, humble reconciliation from the depths of our new hearts…this is the work of human beings loving with the love of Jesus.

We need to realize the Room of Grace is not a pretend fantasyland, full of talking bunnies and rainbow unicorns romping through cotton candy meadows and gumdrop forests. Real people live here, with real problems. They can still hurt, fail, and bear jealousy toward each other. The difference between here and the Room of Good Intentions is what they are learning to believe: that Jesus lives in them, and that they are in Jesus. They are actually righteous, delighted in, and without condemnation even when they do fail. Over time, they actually mature into who God says they are, and they stop hurting each other as often. Slowly, the world around them transforms into a place of safety, trust, freedom, and love, better than anyone could dream. This is not hype or white-knuckled, disciplined resolve.

This is the cure.

Welcome home.

CHAPTER SIX | TWO FRIENDS

"What if it was less important that anything ever gets fixed than that nothing has to be hidden?"

We were kids. We didn't know any better. We just found each other. We learned to play and dream. We told each other everything and made the pacts best friends make. In the confidence of this camaraderie, we risked the deeper woods behind our homes and rode our bikes farther into unexplored neighborhoods. We built forts and dens out in the back alley where packs of us would meet to commune, telling and creating stories. Love was assumed; loyalty and protection were built in. We never went easily into our homes when the streetlights blinked to life. We waited until we were called, and even then only until our parents shouted our full names. We knew when the front door closed behind us, the miraculous world where we were best known, on our level, would be replaced with homework, chores, and bathtubs.

Summer was what we imagined heaven to be. We played hard all day and sprawled on our backs in fields, talking easily about everything and anything. It's where we had our first real conversations about God. We gave unspoken permission for the other to tell hard truth, even badly expressed, because we were convinced the other had our back. We were too young for relational drama or cliques. And if we did get crossways, one glance of acknowledged forgiveness the next morning set us back out into adventures three neighborhoods away. There was little posturing, hardly any deception. None of us knew or cared who was more talented or better looking.

Then a best friend moved away. Or someone stole a baseball card. Or we were split up into rival Little League teams. Or we reached the age when attraction for the opposite sex becomes a competition. Like a chlorine tablet in a summer pool, those childhood communities of trust, safety, and vulnerability gradually dissolved.

What didn't dissolve was our need for them.

Fast forward to now, wherever you're reading these words. For many, looking back means the scattered debris of relationships we thought would always be there, now strained, convoluted, and estranged. We invested our hearts and dreams into those relationships.

We made pacts we'd always face this life together. Our belief in each other was the push to head deeper into the woods of our grown-up world. Then, too many of our friends went away. Almost out of necessity, we grew tougher, guarding our hearts and commitments, giving ourselves an out. Our homes grew quieter. We learned to focus on what our gifting could accomplish. Slowly, without noticing, we closed ourselves off. We're still funny, talented, insightful, but this recording is playing in our heads: *What happened? Why am I unknown, lonely, and lost? Why hasn't this worked out the way I imagined?*

So we dig our own trenches and face increasingly complicated life issues alone. We may meet in small groups, but it's more play-acting than authenticity. We show cracks in measures, with little intention of allowing anyone to help fill them. *Not again. That hurt too much.* Not again.

It feels too late when we awake to discover we learned a theology that fell short of our reality. We learned to place ourselves into comfortable camps or distinguish ourselves from other religious traditions, but we never learned to live with each other in relationships of grace.

One of the most satisfying, visible gifts of the Room of Grace is rediscovering vulnerable, life-giving relationships. We forgot how much we've missed them, how much we've needed them. It's not too late. That life is still there. Jesus never left the fort in the alley. He knows others who are missing those relationships, too. He wants to bring us together again.

·　·　·

I've been here in the Room of Grace, give or take a few hours, nearly six months now.

I can no longer objectively report on life in this new world. I know for sure I see differently now. Don't ask me to explain it. It's like trying to describe a color others have never seen. One can only speak in terms of what the others know, and what they know is not enough to house this new concept: "See, it's, well, sort of like a matted magenta, in a pool of neon-tinted burnt sienna, with rivulets of turquoise almond. It's all kind of fluorescent, but not. You know?"

So, six months. Nothing has stunned me more than the quality and health of the relationships in this room. I knew things would be different with God, and they are, beyond all I'd hoped. But I didn't factor in this part. The way friends interact, protect, and enjoy each other—alongside God—is the most dramatic difference between the Room of Good Intentions and the Room of Grace.

One day, I'm walking the woods, winding up toward a bluff that overlooks the sea with my loud, pajama-clad friend. He likes to walk, and I like to be with him. Neither of us is talking. He walks really fast.

I've known him six months, but our friendship is more authentic and encouraging than any I've known in decades.

I break my panting silence.

"So, you know I'm still a mess. We both know you're more mature than me. Why don't you address my stuff?"

"Hmmm. Would you like me to address your stuff?"

"No, not particularly. But it feels uneasy being around someone who knows your faults and could address them, but doesn't. I'm waiting for a hammer to drop. You do see things in me that could improve, right?"

"Yeah, sure," he shrugs with a smile. "There are all sorts of stuff we see in each other. If it was that simple—just pointing out flaws, and telling someone to fix'em—don't you think we'd all be better by now?"

"Yeah, but…"

"What if it was less important that anything ever gets fixed than that nothing has to be hidden?"[1]

I stop walking, standing in the middle of the trail. The sun is streaming down in beams through the canopy of leaves. It's like one of those religious paintings, only, you know, real. "Say that again. What you just said."

"I said, 'What if it was less important that anything ever gets fixed than that nothing ever has to be hidden?'"

"That's it!" I blurt out. "Those words describe what I haven't been able to say. That's it! Nobody's trying to fix me here."

He gestures forward. "May we walk while you're having this epiphany?"

"No! Just stop for a minute. You have no idea how big this is for me...so, why?"

"Why what?"

"When I was in the Room of Good Intentions, I felt a consistent message everywhere I went, even with all the masks. It went like this: 'There's a bunch wrong with you. We'll give you a pass for a while, but eventually we'll present you with a list of all that needs correcting. The sooner you get fixed, the happier we'll all be.' I couldn't take it anymore. That was the unspoken message that drove me out."

He smiles broadly and folds his arms. "Well, well, well. Listen to you."

"But why?" I continue. "Why is it different here? No one talks about it, but almost everyone lives this way."

"Remember the night I found you wandering back to the Room of Good Intentions?"

I nod.

"There's a way of seeing God in that room. Millions buy into it. It's that whole vision of Jesus 'there' and you 'here,' and your sin a trash heap in between. It's saying you believe you're a saved sinner, who'll always be a saved sinner. Nothing's really been changed in you. Maybe you get some fairy dust, if you beg hard enough. Maybe the Holy Spirit does something. But you are basically a not-very-good person who's trying to be very, very good. You're just a sinner who's going to heaven because of something God did. Not much more. Millions of folks are living their daily lives out of that conviction."

"I saw myself that way for a long time. Still tempted to sometimes."

"Such a picture doesn't buy the astounding reality of Christ in you. Instead, He's 'out there.' It doesn't believe you are actually righteous, only theoretically righteous. To them, you're just righteous enough to get in the gates, but not nearly strong enough to face your own issues. Capiche?"[2]

He doesn't wait for a response.

"So, you're left with the belief that if anything is going to get done, it's going to happen on the wings of willpower and good intentions. It'll happen if only you get serious enough. It sounds noble, but it's like a tar pit. It keeps you stuck in your repetitive mantra: 'I'm not enough.' It can't bring out your new heart. It can only appeal to the broken place in you where sin is given life. The Bible calls it 'the flesh.' It's not your skin, muscle, or anything physical, but a living, active principle inside you, working against you. It has no power to do right. But we appeal to it over and over and over again.[3]

"All along, we have the nature of God fused with us from the moment we put our belief in Him. We have God's love inside us, waiting to be accessed and trusted, available to address our sins and failures, our hopes and dreams. It's all there, untapped, while we're running around trying to impress God with promises and self-denial."

"It sounds like we're taking sin seriously, but it's just the opposite, huh?"

"Yep, just the opposite. Now, in the Room of Grace, there's a different goal, a different motive, a different set of convictions. At the core, we're just learning to trust and depend on our new identity. We're learning to live out of who God says we are on our worst day. So a statement like 'It's less important that anything gets fixed, but that nothing is hidden' is an example of living out of our new identity. It's a realization that sin finds its power when I hide. That nobody gets 'fixed.' That we've already been changed and now get to mature into who we already are. We're starting to discover that this new power is released when we trust it—when I'm safe enough to tell the worst about myself to someone else. See, that's what we're learning to do here. We want to get close enough, be safe and trusted enough, that when that moment comes where God reveals something hard to face, we won't have to run and hide."

"You've done that for me. You know that. Right?"

"Thanks, kid. I sure want to. I wasted a lot of years trying to make people obey and getting obliged compliance instead. Ask my kids. They'd tell you what that gig felt like."

"Say that again."

"Say what again?"

"That part about trying to make people obey and getting compliance instead."

"I think you just said it."

"Right, right. That's another big idea I haven't known. Why don't I know that?"

"Maybe because it wasn't taught or modeled to us. Remember those people you saw camped out along the road after leaving the Room of Good Intentions? That's what they experienced—religious authority figuring out a way to make them obey, appealing to external means instead of the new nature. They tried for so long to oblige, to do the right thing, to make everyone happy. But nobody showed them how to live out of their new nature. They only learned how to look right, how to pacify the demands of someone keeping score. They wanted to obey from the heart, but nobody gave them the chance. Someone was always watching to see if they got out of line, instead of waiting to applaud when they began to trust Christ in them. Eventually they just got disgusted and weary of the game. They stopped playing. Many go their entire lives trying to play this game. They make up the Room of Good Intentions. But those wandering along the path, they just got bitter, or hurt at being played. So they opted out."

"They're the real victims. Aren't they?"

"I guess they are, kid. I guess they are."

"How does anyone ever find their way into anything authentic?"

"Pain, I'm afraid. God allows some pain to awaken our hearts. Many of us are awakening to the pain of realizing we can't control our world the way we thought we could. We're stuck with unresolved issues, symptoms we're trying to fix, without the help of anyone else."

He gestures for us to set off again, so we do, but the pace is slower this time. "Sometimes it's not that you don't want to let others in, but that everyone wants to solve your issues so you won't embarrass them so much. I couldn't find anyone in the Room of Good Intentions willing to stand with me. Everybody just wanted to fix things."

"It's too risky," he says. "They're already beating themselves up for not having their life together. Their shame is so thick you can cut it." He pauses before a slow grin creases his face. "But what if, instead, there was a friend so safe that the worst aspects of me could be known? I would not be loved less but actually loved more by opening up. That thought, my friend, is what broke me open. It was exactly opposite of what I'd always feared."[4]

I let those words hover in the air, like I'm hearing lyrics from an old song, or a quote from a book, that once framed the way I saw life. "For a long time now I've believed if others knew this dark part about me, I'd be pitied and I'd lose my seat at the table. So I just learned to bury those pains, bury those unresolved dark thoughts."

"Except they get buried alive, don't they?"

"So I'm learning."

"So one day I risk it. I think, 'If that's true—if people get to love me more when I let them into my mess—then I have to find some people to try this out with.' I found some. It wasn't an exact science, but I was committed to not giving up. Such a life had to be possible. And over time, I learned it was not just possible, but stunningly real and true. It was God's gift for me to try. It began to reshape my entire life. For the first time, the real me was revealed and enjoyed. I was experiencing love from others. They were allowing me in to protect them! It felt incredible. There were some, are some, even in this room, who didn't know what to do with what I told them. I had to become wiser about who I should trust fully. But today, five years later, I have a community of friends who know the worst about me. They have my back, they carry my shield, and we love each other."

"And then you figured, 'I've got to go find some others who are on the verge of taking that same risk and offer them the same safety.' That's where I come in. Right?"

He says nothing. He only turns to me and smiles with all that is in him. A few steps later, the canopy gives way to raw sunlight and a breathtaking vista of the sea pounding itself against stone and sand. It seems like we can see for miles, and I wonder at how much better the view is when you have a friend to share it with.

. . .

There are two very distinctly different kinds of friends formed by two very distinctly different rooms.

It would be great, at this point, to reflect on those who've had or are attempting to have influence in your life.

Negative influencers will demand your trust of them, as a condition of their support. But it is a trust for their benefit, not yours.

Positive influencers ask permission to earn trust. They will wait for permission to be let in. They put the onus on themselves, not you.

Negative influencers will see you as a sinner who needs help becoming a saint. Their goal will be fixing your issues.

Positive influencers will see you as a saint who still fails. Their goal will be to foster an environment where nothing stays hidden.

Negative influencers will measure your righteousness by how little you sin.

Positive influencers are convinced you are righteous, so they're interested in how you're receiving and giving love. They know that striving to sin less will not mean you love more, but that living in love will mean you are sinning less.

There have probably been people offering direction and insight in your life. But if those positive traits aren't there, you've got the wrong people. They give techniques for controlling behavior, but they won't stand with you in resolving your issues. At best, they'll wield tools for inspiration and a lot of sincerity, at worst, guilt, and performance quotas. They'll make sure you always know who's teaching and who's being taught. They'll rarely risk standing with you in your struggles. They won't truly share themselves with you. At the end of the day, it's all about that person proving his or her superiority before God. It's a notch on a religious belt. Advice and sloganeering are easy and risk-free.

In the Room of Good Intentions, I make you accountable to me so I can control your behavior. The result is that you end up hiding, resenting and mistrusting me. Unresolved issues remain unresolved.

In the Room of Grace, I want to earn your trust so I can love you and be loved by you. The result is that you might want to give me permission to protect you, so you end up hiding nothing in the safety of my commitment. Unresolved issues are brought into the light for healing. Fixing sin is like trying to fix a crimped Slinky. You may think if you just sit on it long enough it might straighten out. Sitting there, you think you've really got a handle on straightening stuff out. But no matter how long you sit, when you get up, that Slinky springs right back. Compromised coiled metal doesn't straighten out by external pressure, and neither does sin.

In the Room of Good Intentions, people are trying to fix others because they've lost the conviction of the power of God's love, the power to live out a new identity. We're afraid grace keeps people from taking things seriously, so we discount the power of love worked out in grace through trust.

Grace is a gift only the non-religious can accept. They're the only ones who can understand it and put it to use. "Religious" folk see grace as soft and weak, so they keep trying to manage their junk with willpower and tenacity. Nothing defines religion quite as well as attempting impossible tasks with limited power, all while pretending that it's working.[5] A healthy friend and protector depends on Christ's life in you to be enough. That way, they can stop policing your behavior and focus on enjoying life in relationship with you.

Somewhere along the line, we became convinced we needed to trade relationships of love for strategic management of others.

That shift frightened us away from each other. That shift forfeited the only distinction Jesus asks us to be known for: loving and allowing ourselves to be loved.[6]

Some of the most disingenuous and useless relationships are those where one has an agenda for another's life, seeing ourselves as scientists seeking a solution for a disease in a twisted lab experiment. These people assume some equation of holiness: Four hours of small group study plus thirty minutes memorizing scripture verses, multiplied by challenge, conviction, and demand make the subject sin less and become a more productive church member. What an absolute travesty of what Christ came for!

God wants us to live authentically—fragile believers, learning to trust Him and each other in relationships intent on love. He wants us out of hiding, acknowledging each other without performance or quotas. He wants us to experience His power healing us as He releases us into a life worth living. This is the Church. This is the Church in the Room of Grace!

THE ENTIRETY OF YOUR LIFE IN CHRIST IS ABOUT LEARNING TO RECEIVE LOVE.

The spiritually immature are not loved well, but it is not because they fail. They are not loved well because they fail to trust the love of another.

Because they trust no one, their needs aren't met.

Because their needs aren't met, they live out of selfishness. Not only do they not receive love, they don't give it either.

In God's eyes, receiving love always comes before giving love. Please read that last sentence again. We have heard too many messages on "learning to love more" or "learning to love better." In truth, we love only when we first learn how to receive the love of God and others. "We love because He first loved us."[7]

But because in the Room of Good Intentions we've been goaded and prodded to love others more, we charge forth to inflict others with our "love."

Real love, however, is always the process of meeting needs. Any other definition is trite Hallmark sentimentality.[8] This is why wearing masks is such a distortion. It causes us to pretend we're enough, without need.

The knowledge that we are loved will never peel away our masks or heal our wounds. "Knowing about love" and "experiencing love" are not the same thing. In the Room of Good Intentions, we will hear a lot about love, and our spirituality may even be assessed by how much we "love" (do for) others. In the Room of Grace, we actually learn to receive the gift of love, to savor it and realize it fully.

The reality of receiving love is so foreign to most of us, we felt the need to include these stages of love.

I UNDERSTAND THAT I HAVE NEEDS.

We might try to ignore this basic requirement because we see needs as weaknesses. We have little problem accepting our need to breathe as imperative for our physical health; having our needs for security, attention and acceptance met is just as necessary for spiritual health. Unresolved sin causes us to define our most innate needs as weaknesses. If we see needs as weaknesses, we'll hide our limitations and call it self-reliance. Or we'll pretend we have no needs and call it independence. Or we'll believe that no one should have to meet our needs and call it strength. Or we'll arrogantly believe we've outgrown our needs as we've gotten more "spiritual." We believe this is maturity, but "I don't need you" is the language of the wounded heart.

I Realize That Having My Needs Met Is Experiencing Love.

Needs give us the capacity to feel loved. We know or experience love when our needs are met. Every day we need to be loved. Every day our God is committed to meeting our needs for attention (God's servant love); acceptance (God's unearned love); security (God's committed love); trust (God's faithful love); guidance (God's directional love); protection (God's jealous love); and significance (God's affirming love). These needs never go away.

I Freely Admit That I Desire to Be Loved.

Many of us have spent years erecting our defenses, building drafty castles stone by stone in the hopes they would safeguard us from the pain of broken relationships. We build them to protect us from pain. Only now are we admitting these walls never really protected us. All they do is keep us isolated and alone. The cost of vulnerability is incredibly high. But what comes next is worth all the risk.

I Choose to Allow You to Love Me.

Only those who risk trusting other flawed people who love them get to experience this love.

I Let You Love Me, On Your Terms, Not Mine.

When first opening ourselves to the love of others, our natural inclination is to demand they love us on our terms: "Do this; buy that; serve me this way." We make others meet the demands of what we think love should look like. In maturing, we discover we don't even know what we need most! Thankfully, God equips others with the ability to meet needs we don't even know exist, in ways we don't even know how to receive.

Will others meet our needs perfectly and will we trust perfectly? Um, no. This is the Room of Grace, remember? "Grace is the face love wears, when it meets imperfection."[9] Learning to love perfectly or trust perfectly is not the point. The point is learning to receive love. Waiting for perfection before we trust people is like expecting prompt service at a closed restaurant. It's just not going to happen.

Instead—and this is the perfect miracle of God—He chooses imperfect friends to love us with His perfect love, all in the journey of perfecting our lives.

I Am Fullfilled When I Have Experienced Love.

Love completely satisfies our longing, ambitions, and potential. God, the ultimate fulfiller, invites us to trust Him. Those who hang out long enough in the Room of Grace experience too much love to return to their previous existence.

Received love turns shaky pretenders into confident dreamers. It turns miserably self-sufficient strivers into wonderfully released receivers. It turns cynical and smug judges into safe and discerning protectors. It turns anxious self-protectors into daring lovers.

I Am Now Able to Love Others Out of My Own Fulfillment.

Having our needs met by receiving the love of God and others is not just about "feeling better"; it's about fulfillment. To fulfill means satisfy, to meet requirements. When the requirements of our needs are met, it satisfies us at our deepest core. This fulfillment produces peace, contentment, and healing. As our wounds heal, we can look away from them with fresh passion, confidence, and love for others.

To give love that can be trusted is the end goal of receiving love. This is where life gets worth living. It jump-starts one of the most profoundly beautiful and miraculous chain reactions anyone gets to witness in this lifetime. Closed, broken, bluffing men and women come squinting out of dark corners and into the light, singing songs and telling stories they didn't know were in them. They begin to feel alive, secure in His embrace, seeing the world for the first time in full color. Each becomes real, safe, creative, and unimpeachable. Almost involuntarily, they begin to offer to all around them a love as rich and freeing as what they are taking in.

Slowly, almost imperceptibly, that miraculous world where we were best known returns, only now even more beautiful. Hurt is transformed into relationships of trusted love. There is unspoken permission for others to tell hard truth, even clumsily expressed. And if you do get crossways, by morning, one glance of acknowledged forgiveness sets you back out riding into awaiting adventures. Now you discover others, many others, are riding with you. Some of them are safe and wildly free, with bikes even more tricked out than your own. Others are broken friendships now restored, more vulnerable and gratefully strong. Some are husbands and wives, once distant and secretly enduring, now riding fully known, grinning alongside each other. Still others held out on the love of Jesus but are now irreparably drawn to Him by the love you've offered. They ride at the front of this pack of friends, risking to go deep into the woods. By day, we work and play hard. At night we lie on our backs in fields, talking unhurriedly about everything and anything. There we have our best conversations about God. There is little posturing, bluffing, hiding, pretending, or deceiving. Few care about who is more talented or better looking.

This is the stunning power of love. This is what Jesus came for us to realize. It is not an illusion or a nostalgic childhood memory. It is ours for the taking.

And the giving.

CHAPTER SEVEN | TWO DESTINIES

"It's God telling you, 'I didn't forget. I made you for this—for the unique influence you have on others. You, my wandering friend, are right on time.'"

I've left the Room of Grace this evening. I didn't tell anyone. I just walked out. Again, I walk the path that skirts along the coast, leading toward the Room of Good Intentions.

But this time I'm grinning like a kid. This time, I'm strolling, drinking in the beauty. I've actually noticed myself whistling. At points along the way, I take running starts to hurl stones out into the night sky, imagining them spinning all the way down the cliffs to the shore. I can't remember the last time I've done anything like this. I'm meandering on and off the path the entire walk, enjoying each new vista and perspective. I'm in no hurry to be anywhere. I have no intention of reaching that gleaming marble edifice looming in the distance. No intention at all.

Instead, I flop down onto a particularly lush outcropping, leaning my back against a giant rock, the moon illuminating a panorama stretching in either direction for miles and miles. The waves are crashing below me and the evening is blanketing me in mist.

I pick this spot intentionally so I can experience being this close to that room without the compulsion to return. I'm surprised to discover I can't feel the difference. How I feel now, full of grace, is normal. It's like trying to remember the feel of oppressive desert heat five days into a vacation at the beach. You can't, really. Where you are just becomes the way it is.

I do wish I had a jacket.

I sit and stare, nearly unaware of time, running my hands along shiny grass, then flipping more stones into the black.

Fourteen months. Hard to believe.

Then, as I toss another stone over the side, I hear a sudden and anguished yelp. "Oww! That hit me!"

I stand up and run, almost involuntarily, to the edge, searching the slope below for who I've wounded.

And there he is. A few feet below but safely off and away from my range: my loud friend. And he is wearing the proudest grin.

I call out to him, shaking my head in feigned indignation. "Really?"

"I couldn't resist," he cries. We both laugh. That loud, long, unembarrassed laugh of friendship.

After he winds his way up to my spot on the bluff, I ask, "Were you worried about me? Is that why you came?"

"No. Not at all." We're both leaning against that rock, looking out at the long stream of reflected moonlight reaching across the ocean. "I wasn't even looking for you. Sometimes, when I can't sleep, I wander out here. I saw you sitting there, tossing rocks, before you could notice me. How could I pass it up?"

"It was brilliant," I nod.

"So, what have you been thinking about out here?"

"Lots of stuff. How long have I been out here? What time is it?"

"A quarter after one," he says, checking his watch. "What kind of stuff?"

I look over at him and back at the ocean. "You know, ever since I was a kid, I've had these dreams."

"Dreams?" He's rubbing sand out from between his toes.

"Not actual dreams, where you're sleeping, but sort of this on-going sense of something that would happen to me someday. Like something would happen that would really matter. You know what I mean? Like I'd be part of something, or get to be in on something important. Growing up, I thought maybe it would be about meeting the right girl, or college, a career. Maybe I thought some mysterious sage with a long beard would show up one evening and whisper, 'Come with me.' He'd drive me someplace and introduce me to a group or a concept or an opportunity that would change the entire course of my life."

"That sounds suspiciously like a cult."

I ignore his playful jab. "I had that sense all the way up until I was maybe twenty-five or so. Then gradually, it went away."

"Why do you think?"

"I've never been sure why. My guess is, I stopped believing God had anything significant for me. That there are certain people whose lives count and I've compromised or squandered my talents enough that nothing significant would ever happen to me."

"I think you just described the private, unspoken despair of millions of people. A dream they once had, of purpose and influence, now muddled into vague survival measures."

"Anyway, sitting here the last several hours, I felt it again."

"Yeah? How does it feel?"

I take a long breath before answering. Things slow down out on a vacant ocean bluff at one in the morning.

"I don't know how to describe it. It's like answering your front door to discover that beautiful high school girlfriend you thought rejected you is now standing there, all these years later, telling you she's still in love. You know?"

"I think I do."

"But it's scary, too. What if nothing happens? What if it's just a fleeting emotion or misplaced nostalgia, and life goes on and nothing ever happens?"

We sit there, both silent for a while, listening to waves break.

"Far be it for me to break up a memory of an old girlfriend, but you want my read?"

"You don't have a long beard, but I guess you'll do." We both smile, both still looking out, transfixed by night's light revealing even the texture of the waves, miles out.

"You know the goal of the Room of Grace was never just about getting healed, right? The goal has always been to free your release into your particular destiny.[1] I have a feeling that's what you're waking up to. It happens to all of us. What you're experiencing tonight, it's real. It's God telling you, 'I didn't forget. I made you for this—for the unique influence you have on others.'[2] You, my wandering friend, are right on time."

"I am?"

"You are. You'll notice this sense didn't come back the first week you got here. You didn't know it, but you found your way to that crossroads, partly because you couldn't live any longer without that hope of destiny. And you couldn't figure out why you kept sabotaging your longing to count, to give your life away."

"I found my way to the crossroads?"

"Your pain did. It allowed you to ask enough hard questions and be open to listening to someone other than yourself for answers. That's when you called out to God. He brought you to the crossroads. But first you had to experience this way of living in your true identity, so you could start healing, so you could mature, so you could be released to love others."

"What now, then?"

He bats at the question with his hand like it's a firefly. "Nobody knows the timing of God. It's complicated, don't you think? But what you sensed tonight? Don't be afraid of it. It's telling you this whole experience is preparing you for a life more beautiful than you could have dreamed."

I can't remember how long it was before either of us spoke another word. I just sat there, not wanting to lose that sense that had been gone so long.

. . .

Philip Yancey asks, "Is it absurd to believe that one human being, a tiny dot on a tiny planet, can make a difference in the history of the universe?"[3] It's not. In fact, that's exactly how God designed His Kingdom. He heals and matures people in order to bring His grace to others who are broken. He uses their gifts, passions, and healing heart to reveal the glory of Jesus.

God has already done much through you, every day since you trusted Him. He does not waste motion, or His choice. This—what the Room of Grace prepares us for—is destiny.

At the very start of this book, we described how many of us feel. We have all these talents, gifts, hopes and dreams we now long to give away for others. But in our immaturity, resulting from our wrong view of God and ourselves, we keep shooting ourselves in the foot. We may have felt,

I carry these dreams I can't shake. Dreams of the part I could play to produce great good. I always thought they were from God.

*I've ached for them to be released. But far more often I hurt and
frustrate the people and environments I long to bless. It's as if
nobody but me can see the dream and there are insurmountable
obstacles at every turn. I may blame others, but I'm pretty sure
most of the obstacles have to do with me. I'm not even sure what
I'm doing to sabotage my efforts. I just do.*

Destiny is what happens when those God-given desires, mixed
with my particular gifting, are allowed to be healed, matured, and
released to freely give away. This is where this whole book has been
heading. This goal, this dream, in this lifetime.

Our destiny is always about loving others, or being prepared
to love others.[4] This is why we need healing so much. Unhealed
wounds require our attention and we will have trouble focusing on
others while those wounds still need attention. This causes many of
us to miss our destinations, on a routine basis, that over a lifetime
produce our destiny.

Destiny is also rooted in the joy of our relationship with Jesus,[5]
which He already purchased for us. When our worldview shifts to
enjoying Him rather than focusing on not sinning, we mature. In
the process of maturing, our eyes open to others and we become
aware of many more opportunities to love than when we focused
on our issues.[6] Destiny is categorically greater than potential. The
apostle Peter appears to have been a pretty mediocre fisherman.
The only time he caught fish, it seems, was when Jesus performed
miracles! But let's say Peter had the talent to catch fish. Maybe, just
maybe, if he'd devoted himself with great passion and dedication,
Peter could have become one of the top four or five fishermen on
the entire Sea of Galilee.

Maybe that was his potential.

But even if he'd accomplished that, it wasn't his destiny. Destiny
is the ordained intention God has sacredly prepared with your name
on it. It is greater than potential like a gold brick is greater than
a microwavable chicken pot pie. Peter's destiny was to become a
fisher of men's hearts.[7] Even today, Peter draws us to God. *That's*
destiny. It wasn't something Peter could manipulate, coerce, or
talent his way into. It's up to God, and it involves His glory, your
fulfillment, and the welfare of others.

God's goal for each of us is never simply healing or safety or rest or even receiving love, as astounding as those gifts may be. His goal is that we'd be released into the sense of purpose we haven't been able to shake all of our lives.[8]

Tragically, not everyone will fully realize the dreams God holds for them. People in the Room of Good Intentions have a hard time finding release into such a life. They're too busy trying to change into who they think God wants them to become, too preoccupied assuaging shame, proving rightness, and polishing worthiness. Every moment of such madness, no matter how slick, keeps them self-centered, immature, and unavailable to others.

Destiny is set in motion when we choose the path of humility.[9] No one knows exactly how God's sovereign intention meshes with our decisions, but there's enough revealed truth to believe they comfortably coexist without damage to either. Maybe it is enough to say the grandeur of our particular destiny is exposed by which room we choose to stay in.

There is no releasing without maturing.
There is no maturing without healing.
There is no healing without receiving gifts of grace.
There are no gifts of grace outside of the Room of Grace.

We who dwell in the Room of Grace have come to believe we are who God says we are. We're not trying to change into someone else. We're not trying to eventually arrive at some higher level.[10] God has formed us exactly the way He wanted, and we've come to believe it. We mature into who we already are, much like a caterpillar matures into a butterfly. We are convinced He wanted us to be here at this exact time, at this exact place, with exactly these personality traits and bents.

That's not to say this is a passive relationship. There is incredible effort in such a journey. It starts with knowing we are loved, complete, and righteous. Jesus taught us our effort will focus not on sinning less, but on loving others. We can strive to sin less, but not love more. But, when we love more, we cannot help but sin less. This effort allows us to extend love to the wounded, angry, and unlovely. It is the effort of actually living out of who He has made us to be.

Jesus matured in God's perfect timing,[11] preparing for the astonishing destiny His Father had for Him.[12] Jesus did not strive to become better. He knew His Father was already pleased with Him.[13] Instead, He trusted His Father.[14] That's the path we should emulate.[15]

Life in the Room of Grace teaches us to wait for God's exaltation rather than to pursue position or power. The timing is perfect. We're no longer in a hurry. For one thing, our dreams are being clarified as our sin is being resolved, our wounds are being healed, and we are in the process of maturing. Our lives are no longer about proving our worth to others through what we get to do. We know He cares even more about our destiny than we do. We know He's already seen the days of our expression.[16]

We're also learning to live with a community of people who trust God and others with what is true about them. We discover we're part of a destiny bigger than our own. While we have an individual destiny, the community we are part of also has a destiny, and we are intertwined with it.[17]

We are not free from problems and issues simply because we no longer hide them. Our issues are exposed to light.[18] We can even appear to have more issues than those in the Room of Good Intentions. We now realize it was wasted energy to cover them.

Maturity in the Room of Grace might best be expressed in three general phases. They overlap, and sometimes we jump back and forth between them. We label them to get a general sense of the intentionality of God to redeem us from self-centered, hidden takers into freed, mature lovers.

HEALING THE WOUNDED

We each enter the Room of Grace self-centered.[19] Soon, though, truth begins to engage our hearts. We become acquainted with the power of love and grace; we begin to recognize the wounds we carry; we embrace our new identity; we discover the treasure of authentic relationships. We also discover the destructive power of unresolved sin. We are immersed in the person of Jesus. We begin to risk the power of the Holy Spirit. We are learning the goodness of the Father.

We will never leave these discoveries, but we'll stagnate and grow cynical if we don't apply the truths we're experiencing. We're going through changes. Friends closest to us are reacting and responding to the changes we're experiencing.

It isn't enough to simply learn what the Bible says about who we are. We need an environment—a community where we see these principles lived out. There must be an opportunity to risk and fail and then experience new life at work. This is how maturity is nurtured.

MATURING THE HEALING

Earlier, the emphasis was on acclimating to our new awareness of truth. Now we are allowing others to join us in our discoveries. We're becoming more outwardly focused. We start applying love, grace and truth to real-life relationships. Our wounds are not just identified; they're being faced.

We're discovering the joy of being with God because we want to, not because we ought to. We're no longer reading the Word as a book of regulations. We read it as the story of our history, who we are now, and what God has in store for us. We read it as free men and women, an integral part of the ongoing story.

We dwell in the realization that love is not something we can drum up, but something now true about us. We begin looking around our community—our friends, family, city, and beyond—to discover opportunities God has prepared since before time began.

We're also introduced to the reality of suffering[20] that results from aligning ourselves with truth. God employs this suffering to mature the humble as we come under His influence. As we grow in trust during this suffering,[21] God expands our influence. We discover others increasingly trust us with truth.

RELEASING THE MATURING

This is that season in which we are increasingly freed into God's destiny for us! We naturally respond to life out of our new Christ-heart. Our past wounds identify us less and less each day.

We now live as intimate friends of Jesus.[22] We are comfortable in His presence. We're done beating ourselves up. We want to be with Him and our heart is free to respond, driven less and less by shame. We mature into a dependence on the Holy Spirit and walk into the purposes of God the Father.

We are owning our influence, making decisions largely for the benefit of others—knowing they are now affected disproportionately by the influence God has given us. We receive our destiny from God's hand.[23] Ah, yes. Destiny. We should probably dispel some misconceptions about how destiny plays out.

* Some wait for their destiny to drop from the sky, accompanied by angels with swords or trumpets. Or both. They may suffer through a painful season and think, *This must have happened so God could move me into the exact, perfect plan He has waited all this time to give me. Hallelujah!* They are waiting more than living, often missing the destiny already being offered day by day.[24]
* Some fear if they don't reach some arbitrary percentage of trust, God will deny them His perfect will of destiny, and they will spend the rest of their days mixing three-bean salads at church functions.
* Some demand destiny from God, calculated by how much they've matured, sacrificed, or come through for Him.
* Some discount the destiny God is performing in them right now, convinced what they've been given is not especially profound. They believe value is determined by the size of

their destiny, by the number of people influenced. They miss what greatness looks like to God. It is tempting to think that if we haven't achieved quantifiable "greatness"—in money, status, influence, etc.—we must have failed in some way to warrant God's full support. This is a cultural distortion of the gospel. It is distinctly Western and bears the damage of fusing destiny with worldly success. God often gives seemingly mundane roles to the most mature, because they are more likely to grasp the stunning intention in even the most obscure responsibility. He will never give you a second-best destiny. He has waited for you since before the world began, and He will never bury His intentions for you.[25]

Much of how you experience this life will stand on how you trust this: The God of all goodness knew exactly where you would be, and planned before time began how He would forge it into good.

Remember that destiny we talked about way back at the start of this journey? Sometimes, destinies do not initiate great new works, or new careers.

Sometimes God says to us, "You get to be the mother of a child who will be very difficult to raise. He'll rebel and break your heart. In his twenties, though, he will return to your love, to God's love. Because of your influence, he will vitally bring lasting transformation to a burned-out, forgotten neighborhood in Nairobi. You will be home with me before this takes form. But we will watch it one day together." Or, "You get to coach a Little League team that improves to 5 and 23 after your first season without a win. But your influence will never be forgotten by the straw-haired second baseman, who came to tryouts without a glove because his single mom didn't even know he was trying out. One day, you will speak to him after practice about the love of God. You will tell him God knows right where he lives and will not forget him. That boy will begin to trust God and make choices that break patterns in his family line. His daughter will develop the technology for a water treatment system, radically increasing life expectancy throughout the world. You will know all of this someday." This is true for all of us:

> *Our destiny is far greater than our potential.*
> *Our destiny is uniquely and perfectly fashioned for us.*
> *Our destiny includes both delight and drudgery.*
> *Our destiny is too important to compromise.*
> *Our destiny is worth sticking around for.*

One more thing: There is often more than one ticket given in your lifetime, more than one scene at the train station. Seasons end, but the conclusion of a particular purpose does not end your destiny. You don't need to figure out when the transition takes place. God can do—will do—all of that. Allow God to reveal the need He has patterned your heart to follow. In the meantime, live fully what is in front of you. Most of us do not discover our ticket in dramatic fashion. We may only know the moment we were sent out in reflection, but a ticket is given, crafted uniquely for you by the loving and sovereign intention of God. He doesn't make mistakes.

. . .

I've been here, in the Room of Grace, for one year and three months, give or take a few hours.

Just a bit ago, I heard a knock at my door. I'm folding clothes, one of my least favorite chores. When I open the door, three people stand in front of me. They are smiling, like they bear gifts they can't wait to give. On the left, the hostess and her husband stand together, and I think back on those moments of intense honesty and authenticity in the coffee shop. They have provided loving wisdom to me ever since. Standing next to them is my best friend. He has irreverently and wonderously modeled friendship and grace, a fount of insight since the moment I arrived. The hostess speaks first. Her words are firm, almost reverent.

"Follow us, please."

We head down the residence wing and out into the great entrance hall. It feels like home now, all that wood and soft cloth and sunlight.

I ask my friends where we are going.

"We don't know. Not all of it," the husband says, clapping me on the back warmly.

They lead me down to the big doors under the banner, and I realize suddenly that I've never been through them. In all the time I've been here, I can't remember even asking where they lead. We pull them open and they swing easily on their hinges, and out of the room cool crisp air rolls over us.

It's dark ahead, and the ceiling is cavernous. This room is even larger than the main hall, with a towering arched ceiling. The hall is thick with a roiling fog of steam, but it seems empty except for the four of us. I can hear a pulsing, idling engine of a train through the cloud.

"What now?" I ask my friends.

"We're not sure. That's for you to find out. You have no idea how we have waited for this day," my friend says, his voice breaking as his eyes well. "I think your part is to just walk forward." I look at the hostess and her husband, and they are grinning, blinking back tears as well. I give them each a hug in turn. I haven't seen my friend this emotional before, but I'm still not sure why or what comes next. He clears his throat and wipes his eyes on a sleeve, choking out the next words, "We are so proud of you." Then the steam rolls over us, enveloping them and they are gone.

There is only the sound of that train, waiting to be boarded. I walk toward the sound through the haze. Soon I can make out the outline of the sleek steel in the mist. But something's wrong. It's subtle at first, then more pronounced. This station is not at all what I expected. I guess I had this picture of some elaborate, ornate, cool-looking, retro train station, all bright, bustling and shiny. Like maybe Grand Central Station in the fifties. But this place is looking and feeling more dingy, gray, insignificant and uncool by the step. This station is not retro, just old and neglected. I'm aware of the growing stench of spoiled, stagnant air, oil, dirt and garbage ground into cement. This station reminds me why people don't ride trains much anymore. I feel ungrateful even entertaining it, but I can't stop thinking, *What if everybody's excited to send me off into a destiny that turns out to be not what I imagined or even want?*

I am now standing, frozen in fear at what my next steps might be taking me into. I have this overwhelming sense I should just turn around and go back to my room. I look back, but there is no one I recognize behind me.

All I can recall are my friend's words, "I think your part is to just walk forward." Walk forward...into what?

Suddenly I remember the day I stood in front of that Trusting God sign after leaving the Room of Good Intentions hours earlier. I remember how little hope I had starting out on that path. So, with the same sigh and a similar tentativeness, I walk forward.

The silhouette of Someone I've come to recognize emerges from the steam—and I smile. The air is still stagnant, the room is just as drab and ugly. But if I've learned nothing else this last year and a half, I know that the Person walking toward me cares for me deeply, makes no mistakes, and probably has a good idea of where I'm about to go.

DISCUSSION GUIDE

Welcome! What a wonderful journey you are about to begin together, embarking on an exhilarating ride to discover or rediscover God's Original Good News. As you meet, we pray you will experience new levels of authenticity as a safe community of trusted love. This is high on God's to-do list for us. He paid everything for us to experience this life of grace. It changes everything!

Take great freedom to make this guide fit your setting and group. Whatever can't be done in this meeting can be finished in whatever ways make the best sense to you. You might want to slow it down and add some additional times together or even go through it again a few months later.

Before you begin, here are just a few guidelines for your time together.

Each chapter contains the following parts:

CHAPTER DISCUSSION

The questions here focus specifically on material from each chapter. Try not to skip over any. Sometimes these truths need to be digested slowly. If needed, take time together to look back in the chapter for those questions that seem challenging.

TAKING OFF THE FILTER

We anticipate this part to be an exciting and freeing time for your group! Together you will learn to discern how the same scripture can be taught from two different perspectives—from the Room of Good Intentions and from the Room of Grace. Each chapter will include a different verse and will ask you to consider it from both perspectives. Sometimes old filters can be hard to take off—so we've included some of our own thoughts in this section to help guide you in this process. We pray this time together will start to form a new way of seeing and understanding God's Word that takes off the distorted filter of "sin-management" theology and allows you to accurately hear what God has lovingly been speaking to you all along.

TO THINK ABOUT

End your time together by reading out loud this last part. The purpose of this part is to leave you with questions or truths to meditate on until your group meets again. While this is meant to be done on your own, we encourage you to also take time to share with each other informally, perhaps outside of your group time, what you may be hearing God say.

At youtube.com/Trueface you can find the video discussion starters used in previous editions.

Finally, we hope you won't see *The Cure* Guide as simply "another study to make your way through," where participants dole out the appropriate religious answers to group questions. Please don't do that. This can be a life-altering experience. This is not merely a seven-week study but an introduction into a way of life. There are no expected answers anyone needs to give. This is an opportunity for you to learn this way of life together. We hope you'll give yourself this great gift! Here we go!

John, Bruce and Bill

DISCUSSION GUIDE
CHAPTER ONE: TWO ROADS

PART 1: CHAPTER DISCUSSION

It's imperative to determine where we're living right now. Give anyone who'd like to a chance to answer this next question:

Which of these three places best describes where you are currently in your relationship with God?

- The Room of Good Intentions
- The Path of Cynical Disillusionment
- The Room of Grace

PART 2: TAKING OFF THE FILTER

Here is that hugely important section where we want to slow down and ponder how we've seen the scriptures, depending upon in which room we've been living. We believe it's critical for us to understand that how we see God and ourselves powerfully affects how we interpret passages. We're convinced many of us have been taught to read the scriptures with man-imposed filters that have prejudiced and distorted the meaning of God's truth.

Your point of view will control what you see and hear from God's Word. If you are standing in the Room of Good Intentions, you will see the same words of the Bible from a different angle than in the Room of Grace. There is an entire world of difference between attempting to obey scripture by goading into self-willed effort instead of appealing to your new nature. In the former you'll infuse the words with pre-embedded messages like "You should be better; try harder to fix yourself; what's wrong with you?" The messages in the Room of Grace are quite different: "You are exactly who I have made you to be; what I am describing in these passages is who you now are, and what you are fully longing and able to live out! This is not a set of impossible standards to beat yourself up with. This is what the new you has waited to get to do."

These biblical reflections are meant as only a starting point. You'll learn to do this with all scripture, even the verses that may have tripped you up, confused you, frightened you or beaten you down. Hopefully we'll eventually get to see all of scripture without the crippling filter.

God does not speak in contradicting voices, based on how much coffee He's had. He has one voice. But our interpretations have often created contradicting voices. It's time for such madness to end.

So, here's this chapter's verse:

"Without faith it is impossible to please God." Hebrews 11:6

How might this verse be emphasized or taught in the Room of Good Intentions?

After you've had a chance to respond, read out loud how we imagine many of us have been taught to see such a verse in the Room of Good Intentions.

All of our insights together will help us grow in learning to recognize when we're seeing timeless truth through dead filters and replace them with life-giving insight.

♦ Are you trying to prove you have enough faith to please Him?

♦ Are you trying to to emphasize all the things you do to

"seek Him"?

♦ Do you create a mental checklist of what's needed to prove your devotion?
♦ Are you in doubt if you're really pleasing Him?

How do you imagine this same verse might be viewed in the Room of Grace?

Read our observations, and listen to hear if our observations start to fit with yours to weave a picture of how God is encouraging us to see this scripture:

♦ Pleasing is a good motive; it simply cannot be our primary motive or we get trapped in Room of Good Intentions interpretation.
♦ Pleasing God is the fruit of trusting God. Pleasing God is also the fruit of godliness, not its root!
♦ God wants our primary motive—our first and last waking thought—to be of trusting Him.
♦ Nothing in the world pleases Him more! If we trust what He says—including whom He says He has made us to be—this pleases Him.
♦ If we trust Him with our life choices instead of trusting ourselves, this pleases Him.
♦ The occupants of the Room of Grace get the privilege of experiencing the pleasure of God, because they have pleased God by choosing to trust Him.

Reading the Bible accurately is at the heart of how an environment is changed. Soon, you'll be asking yourself, in everything you read, "Have I imposed something onto this verse that God never intended? Have I manufactured an attitude, motive or self-condemnation onto this passage that has distorted God's intention?" We're learning how to read the scriptures from the Room of Grace. It changes everything.

PART 3: TO THINK ABOUT

If you are able, find some time alone this week and try to imagine the scenes depicted in chapter one. Recall how you've experienced God when you've failed at something.

1.   What was His expression?

2.   How did you feel in His presence?

Now try to imagine, right after a failure, experiencing Jesus with His arm around you, whispering, "I know. I've known from before the world began. And I'm not ashamed. I'm not angry. I'm crazy about you. I've got your back. I'm here. I love you."

If it feels uncomfortable to view God this way, ask yourself, "Why?" It might be time to risk believing that what Jesus did on the cross purchased not only heaven, but this scene, this relationship, this unmerited affection. Understanding His love this way is intended to give you permission to trust His love every moment of every day for the rest of your life.

Imagine. Believe. Enjoy. Repeat.

DISCUSSION GUIDE
CHAPTER TWO: TWO FACES

PART 1: CHAPTER DISCUSSION

After reading this chapter, give a chance for anyone to answer these questions:

1. How is shame different from guilt?

2. Have you ever felt like shame was driving you to wear a particular mask?

3. How does the Room of Grace make it possible for people to no longer be driven or identified by their shame?

PART 2: TAKING OFF THE FILTER

This process of taking off our old filter might cause us to ask, "Which came first?" The twisted interpretation of scripture that created the lies we tell ourselves, or the lies we tell ourselves creating the twisted interpretation of scripture? It started with the lies we've believed from long before we trusted God. And now we carry those lies into what we presume He'd want to say after we mess things up. We presume He is impatient for us to pull it together on our own, based on our shame.

Here's our next verse:

"Let love be without hypocrisy." Romans 12:9

How would this verse be understood from the Room of Good Intentions?

Let us add to your thoughts. Here's how we imagine many of us to have been taught to see this verse:

- To try and man-up, and push yourself harder to walk the walk.
- Try to will yourself into loving people with more sincerity.
- Think about how much other people in your life need to follow this verse.

How do you think this verse might be taught and emphasized in the Room of Grace?

In the Room of Grace, you might read this verse and:

- Realize that this love is already in you and doesn't have to be added on.
- Decide to relax because Christ is now dwelling in you every moment of every day.
- Discover that living in this identity frees you from wearing masks and lets you experience and share more.
- Delight in the reality that hypocrisy vanishes when you no longer have to hide or pretend you are someone you are supposed to be. Hypocrisy vanishes in the safety of the absolute, unchanging delight of your God and who He says you are.

The scriptures are not describing an impossible list that we'll never quite pull off so that we can get right with Him. Instead, they're describing the very delightfully doable life of one who is right with Him; fully righteous, fused with God and full of the love that meets the only request He gives. Every time we encourage ourselves to read the scriptures, by trusting the new life in us and letting it be wooed out, we are building this new way of living in Him—together!

PART 3: TO THINK ABOUT

It would be great for you to keep asking yourself during this week:

1. How does God want me to live out the unique role He has written for me? Is it really His desire that I "be myself"?

2. If I believe Christ when He says I am righteous and not condemned, is that real and strong enough to keep me from putting on masks?

3. Is there anyone in my life I might risk trusting enough to let them love me more by knowing the real me?

"And when you reach it, unresolved issues will begin to heal. You'll gather up stacks of masks and toss them in the dumpster, brushing your hands together as you walk away. Then, you'll walk out into the daylight, your skin feeling the morning air for the first time since you can remember. You'll drink in the beauty of flowers and earth, free from those nauseating fumes of epoxy holding your face to a mask." (pg. 29)

DISCUSSION GUIDE
CHAPTER THREE: TWO GODS

PART 1: CHAPTER DISCUSSION

We're now at the heart of the journey. Nothing you believe and depend upon is more magnificently liberating than this single truth: You are no longer who you were, even on your worst day. Trusting and leaning upon "Christ in you" is the source of every shred of strength, joy, healing, and peace. What happened in that first moment of trusting Jesus affects everything. This start is called "justification," which means "to be made right."

The difference between seeing God "out there" with me striving to become more righteous, and seeing God "in me" already fully righteous, is the difference between man-made religion and God-infused life. This truth brings freedom to the captives!

As a group, take some time to share your thoughts on the following:

1. Throughout your Christian Life, what have you believed about you actually being righteous?

2. Reflect on the implications of this truth: "Your view of you is the greatest commentary on your view of God." (pg. 34)

3. What difference does it make in your approach to life, whether you are trying to change into who you should be, or maturing into who you are already are?

PART 2: TAKING OFF THE FILTER

Remember, there is a way of seeing in the Room of Good Intentions that slants our interpretation of scripture. Those of us who have only read the Bible through this lens get to challenge our assumptions in the light of unfiltered truth.

Let's look at this verse together:

> *"He made him who knew no sin to be sin on our behalf, so that we might become the righteousness of God in him."* 2 Corinthians 5:21

This is a hugely pivotal verse that has been often obscured. So, let's spend some time examining how the wonder of our actual righteousness, expressed in this verse, might get watered down.

Read our observations first about how this verse might get taught in the Room of Good Intentions.

In the Room of Good Intentions, we might:

- ♦ Presume that Jesus became sin so we would care enough to try to make ourselves more righteous.
- ♦ See the word "might" in this verse as implying that some won't quite get to this righteousness.
- ♦ Believe this righteousness is only legal (theoretical) and not actual.
- ♦ Read these words as a challenge to be more caring based on all He has done for us.

Do our observations connect with what you were thinking? Which ones? Do you have other observations?

How might we see this verse from the Room of Grace?

Read our observations. Understanding this verse in the Room of Grace, you might:

♦ Accept the logic of the argument that in the same way Jesus became actual sin, you actually became righteous.

♦ Upon learning the verb "become" is in a tense meaning once and for all, you could accept that you became righteous at the moment of trusting Jesus, and not as a progressive becoming from self-effort.

♦ Upon discovering that the verb carries no question of doubt, you could accept that, because He became sin on our behalf, you became the righteousness of Christ in Him.

What difference do you imagine it would make if you could believe that you have all of Jesus right now because He lives in you, you live in Him, and you are completely righteous in Him?

PART 3: TO THINK ABOUT

Here are some great verses to dwell on during the week:

♦ Philippians 3:9–10
♦ Galatians 2:20
♦ 2 Corinthians 5:17

Paul says in Philippians 3:10 that he wants to embrace this righteousness and experience Jesus as fully as possible here on Earth. He knows that if he depends in any measure on his own manufactured righteousness, he'll miss intimacy with Christ. How transforming it would be to feel and live the same way!

DISCUSSION GUIDE
CHAPTER FOUR: TWO SOLUTIONS

PART 1: CHAPTER DISCUSSION

By now we're getting a sense of the DNA of an environment of grace, so let's start picturing what it looks like in daily life. It's time to consider how an environment of grace would change the way we view our own sins. In the Room of Good Intentions, we try to control our behavior by self-effort and intense discipline. But it reveals how much we think of our independent ability to face our sin and how little dependence we place upon God's ability to solve our sin.

"Self-protection" might be the most absurdly ridiculous two words ever put together.

It is important to understand how sin can be faced and its power broken in the Room of Grace. This "control cycle" is not limited to certain forms of sin. Every single one of us runs the course of this control cycle at various times and in many varied expressions.

Together as a group, consider the following:

1. How do my unhealthy self-thoughts help fuel this control cycle? (Don't go to the next question until you've taken a stab at this one first.)

2. The power of sin is revealed not when I act out, but in the permission I give myself to act out and not disclose what I'm about to do. Why is it harder for us to admit we're going to do something than it is to admit that I have actually acted out?

3. We say that once this cycle has begun, if at any stage you do not tell another, you will always, inevitably move to the next stage on the cycle. Why do I need you to help protect me in this way?

PART 2: TAKING OFF THE FILTER

Let's continue taking off old filters that we've used in the past to understand scripture.

Consider this verse together:

> *"...confess your sins to one another, and pray for one another, so that you may be healed."* James 5:16

How might this verse get taught poorly in the Room of Good Intentions?

Please read aloud how we think the bias would fall in the room:

- ◆ You'd better or else.
- ◆ A magic formula or technique.
- ◆ Something you do only when you get to the place of really acting out.

How might we see this verse from the Room of Grace?

Here are some of our thoughts on this verse:

- ◆ Confession puts me in touch with Christ's work for all my junk. It is a priceless gift to have His work take care of my sin because none of my own work can heal my sin.
- ◆ Confession heals me from sin issues by letting others into my life so they can love me. Love is one of God's primary healing agents.

- ♦ Confession reminds me that I am a child of the light already, and because of this truth, I can risk living in the light.
- ♦ Confession is an opportunity to call out to others for protection, even when I'm beginning to give myself permission to "go dark" with my sin.

PART 3: TO THINK ABOUT

The power of sin is broken in coming out of hiding.

Very few words have as much power or hope as this sentence above.

It is astounding to discover that God has created others to be our way home when we find ourselves trapped in any area of sin. We have been going it alone for so long, trying bravely to buck-up and fight our way through temptation. When we live this way, we rarely experience the love of others.

We can only be loved when we allow another to meet our needs.

Soak in these two truths this week. Let God direct you into applying them in your present reality. Here's one option: Call the friend you are growing to trust and take him or her out for coffee. Share these truths and your intention to live by them. You'll be giving them part of your life story, just as the hostess shared part of her story in chapter four. Such vulnerability will change and deepen the texture of your friendship and lay the foundation for protection and freedom for the rest of your life.

DISCUSSION GUIDE
CHAPTER FIVE: TWO HEALINGS

PART 1: CHAPTER DISCUSSION

Forgiveness breaks down walls, frees hearts, mends countries, restores families, and draws out the best in us. It can turn hatred into tenderness and the desire to destroy into a passion to protect. It is more powerful than any weapon, government, or wealth. Nothing else can bring such profound healing.

In the Room of Good Intentions, we try to conjure up a forgiveness out of our own willpower, while still deeply wounded and resentful. It never works. We end up faking a relationship. In the Room of Grace, through trusting God's ability, we allow Him to free us from all those barbed hooks keeping us trapped in our bitterness. This is for our sake, to free us, so we can go to the other in authentic love, for their sake. It is one of the most miraculous healings we get to see in this lifetime—someone voluntarily giving pain that has been done to them to the One who can carry it.

Together as a group, consider the following:

1. What does it feel like to be inflamed by another's sin against you?

2. What does it mean that before we can forgive a person horizontally for their sake, we must trust God's protection so we can forgive them vertically for our sake?

3. What's the distinction between forgiving and trusting an offender? How does blurring these two keep us stuck in unforgiveness?

PART 2: TAKING OFF THE FILTER

Here's the next verse to look at together—it ties pretty tightly to this chapter:

> *"...forgiving each other, just as God in Christ also has forgiven you."*
> Ephesians 4:32

How might this verse get taught poorly in the Room of Good Intentions?

We hope it is getting easier to take off those old filters as you read these verses in each chapter.

Here are some of our thoughts on how Ephesians 4:32 might get misinterpreted:

- As a demand because Christ has forgiven you, instead of seeing the "process" nature of the forgiveness you are to extend.
- Meaning "just get over it because Jesus just got over it."

Share how you might now see this verse, standing in the Room of Grace.

Here are our additional thoughts on forgiveness. Take some time to read and react:

- Paul is appealing to my new heart to do what the real me now longs to do—to be freed and released from my own hurt so I can love the one who wronged me.

- ♦ He is describing the nature of the forgiveness exhibited in Jesus, which my new heart can now emulate, because I have the fused love of Christ fully active in me.
- ♦ He is describing how I can be freed from my own bitterness by trusting God to be in charge of defending me in the injustice done to me.

PART 3: TO THINK ABOUT

It would be astoundingly healing to get alone and examine relationships in your life where you've been harboring unforgiveness or unrepentance.

Reread the book chapter.
Then, if and when you're ready, tell God you're tired and weary enough to stop carrying the pain and injustice that's not yours to carry alone, and trust Him with it.

This might be one of the most freeing weeks you'll get to experience in this lifetime. And if you're like many of us, you'll get your life back.

DISCUSSION GUIDE
CHAPTER SIX: TWO FRIENDS

PART 1: CHAPTER DISCUSSION

By now you've read this statement several times: "What if there was a place so safe that the worst of me could be known and I'd discover that I would not be loved less but actually loved more in the telling of it?" In the Room of Good Intentions, well-meaning friends are trying to help get your symptoms fixed. It's often about them not wanting to be embarrassed by your behavior.

The sum effect keeps us on guard, hiding and bluffing. We must change the DNA of the culture. We want to be encouraged into relationships of love, where it's less important that anything gets fixed than that nothing ever has to be hidden.

In a relationship, I must ask myself if I care more about getting issues resolved or establishing a healthy relationship so the issues can be resolved.

In the Room of Good Intentions, I make you accountable to me so I can control your behavior, so you don't embarrass me too much. The result is:

♦ You end up hiding.
♦ You resent and mistrust me.
♦ Your unresolved issues remain unresolved and buried alive!

In the Room of Grace, I want to earn your trust so you'll want to give me permission to protect you. The result is:

♦ You end up hiding less and less.
♦ You trust in the safety of my commitment to you.
♦ Your unresolved issues begin to be resolved and healed because they're in the light!

In your group, share your thoughts on the following:

1. What's the difference between attempting to *fix* issues and *resolving* them?

2. Who do I trust to influence me? Who trusts me to influence them?

3. Read this quote and then discuss together what you think it means:

   "The knowledge we are loved will never peel away our masks or heal our wounds. 'Knowing about love' and 'experiencing love' are not the same thing. In the Room of Good Intentions, we will hear a lot about love, and our spirituality may even be assessed by how much we 'love' (do for) others. In the Room of Grace, we actually learn to receive the gift of love, to savor it and realize it fully." (pg. 76)

4. As you look back through the stages of love outlined in this chapter, what seems most challenging to you? What seems most encouraging?

PART 2: TAKING OFF THE FILTER

Take a look at this next verse:

> *"Bear one another's burdens, and thus fulfill the law of Christ."*
> Galatians 6:2

Hear each other's observations on this verse as seen from the Room of Good Intentions.

Read our takes at how this verse might be seen from this room:

- As trying to keep a law by doing enough "bearing" of other's burdens.
- As a command to "endure" messed-up people.
- As another on a long list of things you aren't doing enough of.

Share a couple responses how you see this verse now from the Room of Grace.

Here are some of ours. Go slowly on these—we think they're pretty important.

- Jesus fulfilled the "law" and gave us the ability to obey Him from the heart.
- This "law" means standing with each other in our hurts, pains, failures, and confusions. It is what Jesus talks about in John 13:34: "A new commandment I give to you, that you love one another, even as I have loved you, that you also love one another."
- This verse gives you an invitation into what most fulfills your new nature. As one who has received love from Jesus

and is receiving love from others, you are freed to stand with friends to love them and protect their hearts.

PART 3: TO THINK ABOUT

Make time this week to ask yourself these questions:

1. Who do I trust to influence me, to know some of the hard, vulnerable things about me? Who do I trust to receive their love?

2. Who trusts me to allow me to influence them, to know some of the hard, vulnerable things about them? Who trusts me to receive my love?

Let those who trust you know how deeply you cherish their love of you. Let them know of your commitment to them.

Let those you trust know how deeply you need their protective love. Be sure to state your permission to them.

DISCUSSION GUIDE
CHAPTER SEVEN: TWO DESTINIES

PART 1: CHAPTER DISCUSSION

By now you're discovering that the ultimate goal of learning how to live in the Room of Grace has never been just about healing. God's ultimate goal is that we be released into the dreams we've not been able to shake all our lives.

God often gives a mundane-looking destiny to the most mature. Because only the mature can trust that around the corner, on a very normal-looking journey, He has some incredibly stunning intention, designed for only you. For the humble, He will never waste your life or give you a second-best destiny. He has waited for you on this planet from before the world began. He will not bury His intention for you now, even if hurt or loss or fear or failure has convinced you otherwise.

Together, share with each other your thoughts on the following:

1. Do you think you are waiting for a destiny that may be already happening?

2. What dream or destiny do you believe God may be forming or currently expressing in you?

PART 2: TAKING OFF THE FILTER

Let's take one last look together at scripture, learning to give ourselves permission to see how God speaks to us, completely righteous believers with new hearts:

> *"For we are his workmanship, created in Christ Jesus for good works, which God prepared beforehand, that we should walk in them."* Ephesians 2:10

First, look at this verse carefully. **How would you imagine we would be taught to live this out in the Room of Good Intentions?**

Read how we've seen the Room of Good Intentions citizens teach this verse:

- ◆ As another in a long series of "shoulds" and "oughts" to do more good works.
- ◆ As a command to go find some more things to do. After all Jesus created us for good works!
- ◆ As an assertion that if you were truly letting God prepare you, you would be doing more good works.
- ◆ As more proof that you aren't walking worthy.

What would we hope to pull from this verse in the Room of Grace?

Here's what we've had the privilege to teach from The Room of Grace:

- ◆ You don't have to drum up these good works; they've actually been prepared from before the world began.

♦ You can have the unspeakable joy of awakening each day to walk into a beautiful life of destiny and purpose He's uniquely planned for you!

♦ You are able to do good works because of who you are now. You have the ability to do what your new heart wants to do!

♦ You have permission to no longer wait for the perfect situation to arrive, but to see destiny being revealed moment by moment right where you are.

PART 3: TO THINK ABOUT

In the midst of your disappointments as well as your hopes, your broken dreams as well as new possibilities, your unresolved issues as well as those God is beginning to heal, read and meditate on this statement each day this week:

> *"Much of how you experience this life will stand on how you trust this: the God of all goodness knew exactly where you would be, and planned before time began how He would forge it into good."* (pg. 90)

It is true for all of us that our destiny is:

♦ Far greater than our potential!
♦ Uniquely and perfectly fashioned for us!
♦ Too important to compromise!
♦ Incredibly worth sticking around for!

You are NOT the exception!
You are NOT the one He forgot to give meaningful destiny to!
He is NOT holding out or playing games with you!

God created you for purpose. He absolutely adores you. He will have His love lived out through you. For this we were made. This is truly our walk across the stage, our time to represent His heart on Earth.

When we get Home, we will see it all revealed in completed wonder. For today, we get to walk out the door and into all the expressions of love customized to all we are from before the world began.

It's time to wrap this series up for now. Before you break up as a group, we wanted to say goodbye. It has been the highest privilege to walk this journey with you.

Remember, you are not alone. There is a growing community all over the world learning these truths of the Original Good News. Many of us are on trueface.org where there are podcasts, courses, events and additional resources to help encourage us all along on this discovery of God's grace!

NOTES

CHAPTER ONE: TWO ROADS

1. Galatians 3:5-6, 11-12.

2. Contrast this sort of mindset with what Paul says in 1 Corinthians 6:9-11 (NASB). He speaks of those among the Corinthian believers who were "fornicators," "idolaters," "adulterers," "effeminate," "homosexuals," and so on, and how they were "washed," "sanctified," and "justified in the name of the Lord Jesus and in the Spirit of our God." Do you think, even for one second, that the readers of that Epistle in Corinth were slyly looking around wondering, "Who are the idolaters? Who are the homosexuals? Who are the swindlers?" No. They all knew these things about themselves—each and every one of them knew the background of each and every other one! And because they knew about these "closet skeletons," they were well equipped to protect each other's weaknesses. That is to say, they knew each other well enough to know where to watch out for each other. They were definitely not living in the land of "Doing Just Fine."

3. Although this sounds so good, there is an important fallacy underlying this statement: the failure to differentiate between our relationship with God and the means to our current fellowship with God. The believer's relationship with God is always that of son to Father. The fact of one's birth creates a permanent relationship with one's parents. Even if a parent wishes to "disown" a child or a child wishes to sever his relationship with a parent, the actual fact of

125

that relationship is inalterable. And, of course, our heavenly Father has promised that He will never leave us nor forsake us. Carrying the human familial analogy further, one might be currently "out of fellowship" with one's children—obviously a painful situation—but they are and always will be his children. In order not to be, they would have to be "unborn." Compare John 1:9-13 and John 10:27-29. The point is that the relationship is, by its very nature, an intimate one. When individuals assume that they can enhance their relationship with God—or their fellowship with God—by working on their sin issues, they are missing the basis for the relationship they have with God, namely the cross. Furthermore, they are missing that it is God who is working with them on their sin issues, because of the cross. It is not them (alone) working on their sin issues in order to "make themselves presentable to God" and, therefore, close to Him.

4. This is akin to living in Romans, chapter 7, and never getting to chapter 8. In the midst of attempting to deal with my sin by trying not to sin, I am living in the reality of Romans 7:15-18: "I do not understand my own actions, for I do not do what I want but I do the very thing I hate.... For I know that nothing good dwells in me, that is in my flesh." I never get to "Thanks be to God through Jesus Christ our Lord" (v. 25). I never arrive at 8:3: "For God has done what the law, weakened by the flesh, could not do." Therefore, our preoccupation with our sin and dealing with our sin keep us anxious about sin, instead of being preoccupied with who God says we are as the basis for dealing with our sin. The good intention of "working on our sin" does not create a redemptive solution, which is the only basis upon which sin can be dealt with. The cross was, is, and always will be God's only way of dealing with sin.

5. 1 Peter 5:6.

6. 2 Corinthians 5:17.

7. Colossians 1:27.

8. Romans 8:9.

9. Romans 7:7–12.

10. Hebrews 11:6 says, "Without faith it is impossible to please God" (NIV). The word "faith" is the noun form of the word "believe" or "trust." Thus, the issue of pleasing God is inextricably bound to trusting Him. What the author is saying is that pleasing God is the result of trusting Him. There is nothing that we can "conjure up" to please Him that is not based upon who He is and what He has already done in and for us. What we mean here by "primary motive" has to do with that which is the driving force of our very hearts. If my desire is primarily to please God, I will be the initiator. I will end up manufacturing all sorts of ways to do this, without reference to trust in the God I'm trying to please. This despite the clear teaching here that nothing I do apart from trust pleases Him. Indeed, James observes that "whatever is not of faith [trust] is sin."

11. Reading something like this often brings specific verses to mind about pleasing God, such as Colossians 1:10: "So as to walk in a manner worthy of the Lord, fully pleasing to Him, bearing fruit in every good work and increasing in the knowledge of God." When we understand this verse to mean that to walk in a manner worthy is an obligation that God intends us to honor by our effort and thereby through strenuous effort we become pleasing to God, we become the judge of how much effort pleases God, and we are quick to judge others for not having enough effort. But if we understand this verse to mean that we are able to walk worthy because we trust who God says we are—saints— then we are pleasing to Him and we are able to bear fruit in

every good work. Note, our effort cannot produce the good fruit. The good fruit comes out of the reality of who we are.

12. Revelation 3:15–22 shows God's response to self-sufficient reliance upon one's own resources. It causes Him to "vomit"! Most translations have made this more polite, using words like "spit," when, in reality, the word means to vomit. Such politeness can mask God's revulsion with such lukewarm self-sufficiency.

13. Hebrews 13:5: "I will never leave you nor forsake you." Many Christians, reading this, would be inclined to say, "Maybe He never leaves but just turns away from us." And they will use a Scripture like 1 John 1:7 to mean that if we are not in the light, He, if not separated from us in disgust, must, in fact, turn from us. And they make the tragic mistake of believing that they now have to do something about their sin to regain His favor instead of believing that He is present with them and is the only resource they have to deal with the sin!

14. Romans 8:1: "Therefore, there is now no condemnation for those who are in Christ Jesus."

CHAPTER TWO: TWO FACES

1. Galatians 3:1–3.

2. This is an example of a distortion of God when truths in Romans 8:31–39 are not believed.

3. 1 Corinthians 3:2–3.

4. Genesis 3:10, NASB, emphasis added. See also verses 6–13.

5. Genesis 3:21: "And the LORD God made for Adam and for his wife garments of skins and clothed them."

6. Titus 3:5–6.

7. Ephesians 1:6, KJV.

8. See Revelation 3:17. Some of you may be thinking, "Well, I definitely don't think we are in the Laodicean period!" Whatever your eschatological views about Revelation 2–3 are, please recall that the seven churches to whom John wrote on behalf of Christ Himself were seven actual churches in seven actual cities in Asia Minor. The question to ask yourself is, "Do I sound like the Laodiceans with their smug self-sufficiency?" "For you say, 'I am rich, I have prospered, and I need nothing.'"

9. Psalm 51:3–14.

10. Psalms 31:12; 41:7–10; 52:2–4; Proverbs 15:4; 25:28; 27:4.

11. There are many biblical illustrations of these truths. Look, for example, at the events in 1 Samuel 25 between Nabal and David. David dispatched his men with a reasonable request for Nabal. Nabal (whose very name means "fool") responded harshly and ungraciously. David's (natural) response was to avenge the affront of Nabal. Nabal's wife, Abigail, however, intervened with grace, charm, and intelligence. In doing so, she not only averted David's wrath against Nabal, but also gave place for God's righteous judgment against him. Compare this sequence of events with Romans 12:19-21.

12. James 1:22–24.

13. 2 Corinthians 3:18.

CHAPTER THREE: TWO GODS

1. This is reminiscent of seeing and believing Romans 8:31, for example, for the first time and thinking, "Life will never be the same again!"

2. Genesis 3:10. Adam and Eve, now aware of their nakedness because of their shame, hid from God, because they were afraid. This is not the healthy "fear of the Lord" spoken of in Proverbs and elsewhere. This is being afraid of God.

3. Luke 18:9–14.

4. John 15:4.

5. John 17:21.

6. 2 Corinthians 5:17.

7. Romans 12:1–2. Paul specifically references this truth in that he uses the word "transformed." It is a form of the Greek verb from which we get "metamorphosis," which is nothing other than the process of maturing into what we were designed to be. The DNA of the caterpillar is precisely that of the butterfly that will emerge from its chrysalis. It has simply "metamorphosed" into that which it was designed to be.

8. Ephesians 4:24; 2 Peter 1:3.

9. As part of our new creation, it is imperative that we believe we have a new heart (Romans 6:17). If I am still believing that my heart is deceitfully wicked, there is no way I will ever trust that I am who God says I am. And I will live unable to trust my new heart not to try to take advantage of God.

10. Romans 5:19: "For as by one man's disobedience the many were made sinners, so by one man's obedience the many will be made righteous." Like the reality of our being sinners in fact in Adam's disobedience, we are made righteous in fact in Christ's obedience. Some, believing that their righteousness is only a right standing before God, would never take the position that they are only a sinner in their standing before God. To be consistent, I am both a sinner in fact and before God, and I am righteous in fact and before God. See 2 Corinthians 5.21; Ephesians 4:24; Philippians 3:9; Romans 6:18; plus the dozens of references to the fact that we are "saints," holy ones. Those who would make our righteousness merely forensic miss the impact of all of these verses.

11. In John chapters 13 through 17 Jesus teaches a new theology to His disciples regarding who they are, their relationship with God, and their future destiny. He gives them a new commandment to love. The old commandments demonstrated the unrighteousness of man. The new commandment to love demonstrates a righteousness in the believer because of Calvary. Jesus teaches that He and the Father will abide in them and they will abide in Him and in the Father. Prior to Jesus' teaching, God dwelt among Israel in a tabernacle and a temple. Because they were not yet righteous, He could not dwell in them. Jesus teaches that the Holy Spirit will be in them, whereas prior to this, the Holy Spirit could only "come upon" man. Because of Calvary and because the disciples will be made new—righteous— the Holy Spirit can dwell in them, not just upon them. He also taught of the reality of the rich man and Lazarus. In that reality, the imputed righteous believers of the Old Covenant were not yet able to go into heaven until Jesus, after His crucifixion, went into paradise to release them, because now, like the New Testament believer, they are fully righteous and can dwell with God.

12. Galatians 5:1, 13-14. Understand who God has created us

to be: Paul's teaching on freedom is not from sin but to something. It is the freedom of those who are free now to go about life in a free manner. When we miss this point, we look for individual sins that we're free from, but get trapped into a "management" of sin that robs us of the freedom of who we are. How much better to live in the freedom of love than to try to live free from sin!

13. Colossians 2:9–10.

14. Colossians 4:12: "That you may stand mature and fully assured in all the will of God."

15. Galatians 3:1–3. Paul's argument here centers not upon the Galatians' incorrect view of their justification, but of their sanctification. They missed who God really is and went back into a system that could not give them life or hope. By the way, Paul called them foolish.

16. Romans 8:1: "There is therefore now no condemnation to those who are in Christ Jesus." For those who for years have lived in the agony of their shame—because of their choices or the choices made against them—there is probably no verse that offers them greater hope than to believe that, because they are new in Christ, they are no longer identified by their shame. They are, in fact, no longer condemned. If a person is unable to believe that, he or she will remain self-condemned and live out of that self-condemnation in an effort to be accepted or acceptable, or will stop trying and lose all hope. This is one of those places where our opinion of ourselves has to change to God's opinion of us. If we are unable to believe who we are in Jesus, and to live out of who we are, we will remain convinced that we and all others are unacceptable, condemned.

CHAPTER FOUR: TWO SOLUTIONS

1. Romans 7:18-20. The root of her reality is that we, as saints, have flesh. Grace never ignores this reality, but is the only resolution to it.

2. James 1:13-15 outlines the process: temptation, carried away, enticed by lust, planting of the seed of sin, birth of sin, equals death. Although sin would be delighted if this always ended in the physical death of the believer, it is satisfied with the death of a relationship, love, and hope. We must be aware of this dynamic.

3. Proverbs 2:11-15.

4. 2 Samuel 11:14-15: "In the morning, David wrote a letter to Joab and sent it by the hand of Uriah. In the letter he wrote, 'Set Uriah in the forefront of the hardest fighting, and then draw back from him, that he may be struck down and die.'" Obviously, David thought he could deal with the consequences of his sin.

5. Genesis 3:12: "The man said, 'The woman whom you gave to be with me, she gave me fruit of the tree and I ate.'"

6. 1 Samuel 13:11-12: "Samuel said, 'What have you done?' And Saul said, '... I saw that the people were scattering from me and that you did not come within the appointed days...so I forced myself'" (emphasis added).

7. Romans 7:24-25: "Wretched man that I am! Who will deliver me from this body of death? Thanks be to God through Jesus Christ our Lord!" This is the cry of an apostle of Jesus Christ, the founder of many of the churches in the New Testament, the author of much of your New Testament!

Paul, the writer of the truths of God's grace, confesses the reality of his flesh and wrote, "for I know that nothing good dwells in me, that is in my flesh" (Romans 7:18). He wrote, "If by the Spirit you put to death the deeds of the body, you will live" (Romans 8:13). An understanding of grace is always an understanding that our Christian life is not about living as if we do not sin; it is living in the hope and power of the provisions of God when we sin.

8.   Romans 7:25: "With my flesh I serve the law of sin."

9.   2 Samuel 11. With multiple wives and concubines, David wasn't lacking sexual attention. His "need" for Bathsheba was purely to satisfy his sinful nature.

10. Ephesians 5:8-14: "For at one time you were darkness, but now you are light in the Lord. Walk as children of light" (v. 8).

11. Galatians 6:1-2: "Bear one another's burdens and so fulfill the Law of Christ" (v. 2). As a reminder, the Law of Christ is to love one another as He has loved us. There is no experiencing love without being vulnerable to those we trust.

CHAPTER FIVE: TWO HEALINGS

1.   2 Samuel 13. Examine Absalom's response to the hurt done to his sister by Amnon: "But Absalom did not speak to Amnon either good or bad; for Absalom hated Amnon because he had violated his sister Tamar" (v. 22, NASB). Then he proceeded to plot and carry out Amnon's death! This offense also set up the heart attitude of Absalom that later resulted in his rebellion against his father, David.

2. The truth is that He is for you! Romans 8:31: "If God is for us, who can be against us?" (NIV).

3. 1 Peter 5:5-6.

4. Every act of trust is an act of humility. In an act of humility (trusting) I am vulnerable, and I am promised God's grace. 1 Corinthians 13:7 says that love "always trusts" (NIV). Many live believing that only God can be trusted and, therefore, they don't have to trust anyone else. Until they realize that their choice to not trust (which is a decision to not be humble before others), they will continue to be robbed of their greatest need—to be loved. There is simply no way to experience love without trust. Therefore, their decision to not trust others, because they don't have to, is to disobey the clearest commandment of Jesus, "Love one another."

5. Ephesians 4:32.

6. Hebrews 12:15: "See to it that no one fails to obtain the grace of God; that no 'root of bitterness' springs up and causes trouble and by it many become defiled." In The Message, Peterson says, "Keep a sharp eye out for weeds of bitter discontent. A thistle or two gone to seed can ruin a whole garden in no time."

7. 1 John 1:7: "The blood of Jesus His Son cleanses us from all sin." Unfortunately, many have been taught that this is the cleansing power of the cross for sins we have done, without carefully noting that God is capable of cleansing us from all the sin done to us as well. If we miss this point, we will misunderstand how absolutely necessary forgiveness is for our sake. I cannot live well with the unresolved, uncleansed effects of sin done against me.

8. 2 Timothy 2:25 (NASB).

9. 1 Peter 1:17-19.

10. For instance, see 1 Peter 2:21-24, where Peter tells us that Jesus Himself, in the midst of His suffering in our place, "kept entrusting Himself to Him who judges righteously" (NASB). If anyone could ever have stamped His foot and decried the injustice, it was surely Jesus at that moment. Instead, He trusted the Father.

11. In Luke 23:34, Jesus did not deny the actuality of the wrongs done against Him, but rather asked the Father to forgive those wrongs—for Jesus' sake. The wrongdoers had not repented, yet He forgave them.

12. Hebrews 9:11-14, 22, 26-28.

CHAPTER SIX: TWO FRIENDS

1. 1 John 1:5-7: "This is the message we have heard from Him and announce to you, that God is Light, and in Him there is no darkness at all. If we say that we have fellowship with Him and yet walk in the darkness, we lie and do not practice the truth; but if we walk in the Light as He Himself is in the Light, we have fellowship with one another, and the blood of Jesus His Son cleanses us from all sin" (NASB). There are several remarkable observations one can make about this passage, but let's just concentrate on a few. First, John does not say that if we walk in the light as He himself is in the light, we have fellowship with Him. But isn't that what we would have expected? Of course, we have fellowship with Him if we're walking in the light. The unexpected thing—the really astonishing thing—is that we can now have fellowship with one another! Furthermore, that is the natural result of walking with Him in the light. As if that were not enough of a surprise, John goes on to say

that this walking-in-the-light-fellowshipping process also results in the blood of Jesus continuing to cleanse us from all sin (the present tense of the verb indicates a durative—an ongoing—aspect to it). In other words, walking in the light—with nothing hidden—results in genuine fellowship and in a continuous cleansing that is based upon Christ's finished work on Calvary.

2. See, for example, Colossians 1:9-13. This extended passage, apart from being one often cited by those who advocate pleasing God over trusting God, clearly indicates that God has "qualified us to share in the inheritance of the saints in Light" (NASB). Paul goes on to say that God "rescued us from the domain of darkness, and transferred us to the kingdom of His beloved Son" (NASB). Somehow God has changed us so profoundly that we have actually changed realms! The one to whom we owe our loyalty has changed. We used to be a part of Satan's kingdom; now we are a part of Christ's. That sounds like a good deal more than something that is "merely forensic." It sounds like an actual change of nature.

3. Romans 7:14, 18, 21.

4. 1 Peter 5:5 talks about clothing ourselves with humility toward one another. Few things are as indicative of true humility as allowing ourselves to be seen—really seen—by our brothers and sisters in Christ. Allowing oneself to be seen "warts and all" indicates one's willingness to trust others to protect one's weaknesses. Anything else, it can be argued, is pretense—or lack of humility. And, as Peter reminds us, that is called "pride." "God is opposed to the proud, but gives grace to the humble."

5. Once again, see Galatians 3:1-3.

6. John 13:34-35.

7. 1 John 4:19.

8. John 3:16, probably the best-known verse in the New Testament, illustrates the truth of this. It says, "God so loved the world that he gave..." The little word translated "so" here does not mean "so much," although that is how most read and understand it. It actually means, "in this manner; in this way." In other words, John says that God loved the world in this way, that He gave His only begotten Son that whoever believes in Him will not perish, but have eternal life. God saw our crying need—that we stood already condemned (see verse 18) before the Holy God. He loved us in that He gave His only Son to meet that need.

9. Joseph R. Cooke, *Free for the Taking: The Life-changing Power of Grace* (Old Tappan, NJ: Revell, 1975), p. 7.

CHAPTER SEVEN: TWO DESTINIES

1. In Colossians 1:21-22 Paul points out that the actual reason why Christ reconciled us is in order to present us holy and blameless and beyond reproach to the Father!

2. Colossians 1:23.

3. Philip Yancey, *Disappointment with God* (Grand Rapids, MI., Zondervan, 1988), p. 169.

4. Galatians 5:6.

5. Psalm 16:11.

6. Matthew 9:35-38; Philippians 1:3-11; Colossians 1:9-14.

7. Matthew 4:19-20.

8. Ephesians 2:10. God has tailor-made good works for you to perform! They're out there waiting just for you.

9. 1 Peter 1:5-6 and Philippians 2:5-11.

10. Colossians 2:1-3.

11. Hebrews 5:7-9.

12. Hebrews 12:1-2.

13. Matthew 3:17.

14. John 13:3-4.

15. 1 Corinthians 11:1.

16. Jeremiah 29:11. God delivered this promise to Israel even after seventy years of exile in Babylon! He still had remarkable plans for them. He does for you too!

17. 2 Thessalonians 1:3-4.

18. Ephesians 5:7-9.

19. 1 Corinthians 3:1-4.

20. 1 Peter 3:14.

21. 1 Peter 2:21-23.

22. John 15:13-15.

23. Many have benefited by placing these three phases within the timeline exercise suggested by Dr. J. Robert Clinton in *The Making of a Leader* (Colorado Springs, CO: NavPress, 1988) and in his other works.

24. "Give your entire attention to what God is doing right now, and don't get worked up about what may or may not happen tomorrow. God will help you deal with whatever hard things come up when the time comes" Matthew 6:34 (MSG).

25. Those who define "destiny" by earthly success conclude that the people of faith in the first half of Hebrews 11, like Abraham, Moses, Rahab, were more valuable, important, or blessed by God than those in the second half of Hebrews 11, because those in the first half got to do "big things" and those in the second half were tortured and killed. Yet, it is clear those in Hebrews 11:35–40 pleased God because they trusted Him, and God commended them. The writer of Hebrews says "the world was not worthy of them" and they received "something better" than what was promised. Such was the great reward of their destiny.

ACKNOWLEDGMENTS

All over the world, a company of people stand with us, loving us in our vulnerability, earning our trust, so they can give us wisdom and influence to strengthen our ability to accurately speak and live this gospel of God's grace.

Countless thousands encourage us simply by living out the life we are attempting to paint. They form a community that folds in and out of hundreds of businesses, universities, churches, families, individuals, ministries, media outlets, coalitions and organizations. They are musicians, authors, theologians, counselors, doctors, pastors, students, journalists, educators, missionaries, politicians, professional coaches and athletes, homemakers, executives…and addicts, the incarcerated, victims of trafficking, the estranged, failed and defrocked leaders, the ideologically oppressed. They represent all ages, and transcend all cultures, ideologies, age, gender and ethnicity. We write and speak with them.

We continue to be grateful beyond words to our Board member families, Advisory Council and Friends of Trueface. They have sacrificed everything from resources to schedules, and stand arm in arm with us in this message of God's redemption, grace and destiny. We call on them often to encourage us, pray for us, and direct us in learning how to more effectively get this ancient message to the world.

The excellent staff team of Trueface has, from the very beginning, faithfully figured out how to keep this community thriving. They are not employees, but servants committed to risk this life we are promising.

From the very beginning, we have deeply appreciated our dear friend Stewart Black, a gifted theologian who expresses the message of this book through his life and teaching, and has helped us clarify the biblical endnotes of *The Cure*.

Then there are many churches and institutions that continue to heroically hold to this grand experiment of grace and identity in Christ.

Jordan Green (www.burnsideeditorial.com) has been our superb developmental editor. How grateful we are that our paths crossed with Jordan just before *The Cure* began its editorial journey.

Bob Bernatz is a corporate psychologist and entrepreneur who keeps pressing us to believe this message is bigger and more important than even we are describing it. He gave us language to describe one type of mask wearers in the Two Faces chapter. He also convinces us that those who don't yet know God need this book vitally.

Our wives especially have owned the cost of carrying this gospel message, which is being rediscovered in this stage of history. Thank you, Stacey, thank you, Janet, thank you, Grace.

Oh, by the way, the three of us, John, Bruce, and Bill, still love, respect, and protect each other. The relational waters are not always smooth, as we three create a team of very different and strong personalities. But, God has kept His hand on us these past twenty years.

ABOUT THE AUTHORS

JOHN LYNCH

As a world-class communicator, John is a vital Trueface staff member. In addition to speaking internationally with the Trueface team since 1997, John has co-authored *The Cure, Bo's Café, Behind the Mask,* and his own story, *On My Worst Day.* John also powerfully delivered the classic *Two Roads, Two Rooms* allegory, which the co-authors created for *The Cure.* This message can be heard or seen on the Internet.

John served for 27 years as teaching pastor at Open Door Fellowship in Phoenix, Arizona. John used his love for theater as a playwright and actor in Sharkey Productions, a troupe focused on gospel-anchored theater productions for those still seeking Jesus.

John and his wife, Stacey often create inviting environments on their backyard patio and elsewhere for people to enjoy authentic community. They are passionate parents to their three children, Caleb married to Kali, with granddaughters Maci and Payton; Amy married to Cody, with grandson Ridge and granddaughter Navy; and Carly.

BRUCE McNICOL

God has used the teaching, wisdom, global vision, and business skills of co-founder and president Dr. Bruce McNicol to help Trueface offer breakthrough experiences of grace for many thousands around the world. Leaders in all spheres of influence have found God's lasting resolution for their life issues and key relationships as they have journeyed with Bruce.

With degrees in finance law, theology, leadership and organizational development, Bruce's gifting to write to diverse readers and leaders has proved true in the bestsellers he has co-authored: *The Cure, The Ascent of a Leader, Bo's Café, Behind the Mask, The Kingdom Life,* and *High Trust Cultures.* Audiences in various countries continue discovering hope and freedom from Bruce's story-driven, biblically anchored teaching.

Having lived in Portland, Los Angeles, San Francisco Bay Area, Chicago, and Phoenix, Bruce has gained a variety of interests through the years, including international cultural trends and needs, music, hiking, reading, comedy, and sports. His constant interest is his wife, Janet, who is a homemaker, nurse, and mentor. Bruce and Janet have received extensive tutoring from their three wonderful children and spouses: Nicole, married to Kory, with grandchildren Willo and Elliott; Chad married to Erica; and Ryan.

BILL THRALL

As co-founder of Trueface in 1995, Bill's wisdom has been penned throughout *The Cure, The Ascent of a Leader, Bo's Café, Behind the Mask,* and *High Trust Cultures.*

Bill's gifts and experience also shine as he helps leaders establish trust in all their key relationships and nurtures grace-based environments. CEOs of international companies to heads of mission organizations and universities have repeatedly discovered a lifelong gratitude for spending time with Bill.

Prior to joining Trueface, Bill founded and pastored Open Door Fellowship for over 20 years. While there he developed an effective character development training program, which nurtured visionaries such as Kit Danley, founder of Neighborhood Ministries.

In his spare time, Bill can be found fishing, golfing, crafting furniture for his family in his woodshop, and cultivating fruits, herbs, and vegetables in his fertile backyard garden. Bill and his wife, Grace, have three grown children; Wende married to Jim; Bill married to Charlotte; and Joy married to Joe; and nine grandchildren.

If you've been touched by the imaginative freedom of
this story and want to help make it available to others at
a wider level, we invite you to participate in...

THE CURE PROJECT

Word of mouth is still the most effective tool for a book like this to gain a hearing in the culture.

Give the book to friends, even acquaintances, as a gift. They will not only experience an exhilarating journey but also get a glimpse of the true face of God.

To order go to Trueface.org. *The Cure* is also available on all ebook formats, including Kindle and as an audio book.

Please feel free to leave us a review on Amazon, or if you have a Facebook page, blog, or website, consider sharing about the book.

If you own a shop or business, consider putting a display of these books on your counter to resell to customers. Or buy a set of books for prisons, women's shelters, and rehabilitation homes, where people can discover hope and joy in the cure.

Follow us on Instagram: @truefacelife
"Like" our Facebook fan page: facebook.com/TruefaceCommunity
Small Group & Churchwide Series resources available at: Trueface.org

Thank you for being a carrier of the cure with us,
John, Bruce & Bill

THE TRUEFACE MISSION

trueface.org Carriers of The Cure

Trueface is part of a global movement to see millions of high-trust communities of grace multiplied around the world—because we believe Grace Changes Everything!

Grace changes how we read the Bible and trust its truths. Grace changes how we see the true face of Jesus, and our desire to follow Him. Grace changes how we heal, mature, and live out the dreams God has for us. Grace alters how we create safe environments in our marriages, families, and friendships. Grace changes how we resolve prejudice, discrimination, and oppression. Grace changes how we handle conflict, sin, anger, addiction, shame, and failure. Grace changes how we forgive, repent, and develop emotionally healthy relationships. Grace reshapes our schools, businesses, and governments. Grace changes how we develop leaders, and their teams, and inspire their best work. Grace changes us into generous people. Grace changes how we teach, motivate, disciple, and inspire our faith communities. Grace changes how we lead people to Jesus and influence society. Most importantly, grace changes how we see God, ourselves, and others.

Grace changes everything!

If you would like to explore more about how grace changes everything, we invite you to step into the Trueface mission, where we help people experience grace in relationship. We do this by offering safe places to trust God and others with you. To help restore this original good news to you Trueface offers a variety of means for your journey, including books, study guides, events, videos, podcasts and other social media, group online education, consulting, and partnerships. In this relational process, we believe you will discover the true face of Jesus, again—maybe for the first time—He is the source of every high-trust community of grace.

Contact us at INFO@TRUEFACE.ORG

OTHER BOOKS FROM TRUEFACE

 The Cure & Parents

 Bo's Café

 The Ascent of a Leader

 Behind the Mask

 On My Worst Day

 Lay It Down

 Trust for today

 The Heart of Man